The Computer Science Research of James Alan Riechel:

Search, Sort, and Other Topics (2007—2014)

by James Alan Riechel

Table of Contents

I. Failure-based Reasoning

Failure-based reasoning

James A. Riechel*

November 2, 2007

Abstract

We solve the game of tic-tac-toe using a case-based reasoning system, where a database of failed game positions or boards, and their immediate and obvious moves which led to failure, are maintained. The system begins with a null or empty database of failures, and only a single heuristic is implicit in our case-based reasoning system: play random moves excluding moves in our failure database which led to failure in the past. The system plays itself, alternatively playing moves for both X and O, and the failure database increases in size until it becomes stable and the game of tic-tac-toe is "solved."

1   Introduction

The hidden complexity of an apparently simple game like tic-tac-toe makes the game a valid subject for research in artificial intelligence. One measure of complexity in the domain of games is the number of unique games that can be played from the starting position to all possible end positions following the legal rules of the game. Probability theory, discrete mathematics, and combinatorics can measure this complexity of tic-tac-toe, given one assumption. We assume that all games complete with no unoccupied squares, even if 'X' or 'O' achieves an early victory before all nine squares are occupied. Given this assumption, there are

$$\binom{9}{5} 5! \binom{4}{4} 4! = 9! = 362,880$$

possible and unique games of tic-tac-toe. Over the course of a game, 'X' chooses five squares to play in out of nine, and he can choose to play those five moves in any order. Over the courses of a game, 'O' chooses four squares to play in out of the four remaining squares available to him, and he can choose to play those four moves in any order. There are exactly 362,880 possible and unique games of tic-tac-toe. A number of this order of magnitude is today considered tractable by computer scientists, but artificial intelligence research in tic-tac-toe is appropriate because it is both tractable and sufficiently complex.

---

*jamesriechel@gmail.com

2 Methodology

Our system employs no explicit heuristic to aim for any particular result in tic-tac-toe. It plays neither to win, lose, or to draw. Also, no type of search algorithm is used to aid in the selection of a move. The system knows how to play a legal game of tic-tac-toe, and the system knows whether the current game is still in progress, whether the current game has ended in a tie-game or draw, whether the current game has finished with 'X' as the victor, or whether the current game has ended with 'O' as the victor.

When a game is lost, or when a loss is unavoidable, a failure assignment is made. The failure assignment identifies the losing move in the critical position in which the losing move was made. The critical position and the losing move made in the critical position are added to the failure database.

On any given turn in any particular game of tic-tac-toe, whether it is X's turn to play, or whether it is O's turn to play, we generate all possible legal moves for the current player. From this list of all possible legal moves, moves which have led to failure in the past are excluded. Only a simple search of the failure database is required to exclude these moves. In this manner, our system, as best as possible, avoids failure. Failure in the context of tic-tac-toe is, of course, loss of the current game by the current player. Of the remaining available moves for play which have not led to failure in the past, one is chosen randomly and played.

2.1 Failure assignment

When a game is lost, or when loss is unavoidable, we identify the critical position and the losing move made in the critical position which led to the loss. The critical position and its losing move are then added to the failure database. There are two types of failure in tic-tac-toe. First, if a move is played, and then the opponent plays a move which immediately wins, the move which allowed the opponent to win is identified as a failure and added to the failure database along with the critical position. Second, if the current player has no moves available which don't lead to failure, then the previous move by the same player is identified as a failure and added to the failure database along with the critical position.

2.2 Choice of move

Given a current game or tic-tac-toe board, we first generate all possible legal moves for the current player. Next, for each possible and legal move available for play by the current player, we compare the current board and the current move under consideration to determine if the current board and the current move under consideration appear as a failure in the failure database. If the current board and the current move under consideration appear as a failure in the failure database, we exclude the current move under consideration as a choice for play.

If, as a result of this process, the current player is left will no moves which will not lead to failure, we record the last move by the current player as a failure, and regenerate the full list of legal moves for the current player, even though all of them have been previously identified by the system as failures. The system does not "resign," and the game continues. It is possible that even though all moves could lead to failure, the opponent may choose to draw instead. The system, alternatively playing moves for both 'X' and 'O', chooses random moves which have not led to failure in the past. If we assume the failure database represents all possible failures in tic-tac-toe, the system playing either for 'X' or for 'O', plays for a draw or better. A draw in tic-tac-toe is, of course, a tie-game, or what children call a "cat's game." Our system employs a failure-avoidance strategy. It may not always avoid loss, but, as best as possible, it plays for a draw or better.

So, legal and possible moves for the current player are excluded and possibly re-introduced as described above. Of the moves that remain, one is chosen randomly and played.

3 Implementation

In all cases, our system beings with an empty or null database of failures. The system then plays a specified number of games of tic-tac-toe, alternatively playing moves for 'X' and 'O' until each game is complete. If a game ends in a failure, that is, if either 'X' wins or 'O' wins, or a loss by 'X' or by 'O' is unavoidable, the critical position and the losing move made in the critical position are identified and added to the failure database.

Running statistics are collected and maintained, including: the total number of games, the number of tie-games, the number of times a game ends with 'X' as the victor, the number of times a game ends with 'O' as the victor, and the number of times a possible failure was avoided by excluding a move from play that might lead to failure. After all games are played, the failure database is written to a file, and the size of the failure database is reported along with the other running statistics.

4 Some theory

There are some theoretical bounds on the size of the failure database our system can create. 'X' has nine choices for play on his first move, 'O' has eight choices for play on his first move on a board that already has one 'X' placed in one of the nine squares, etc. Now assume that for the game of tic-tac-toe there exists a ratio $r \in [0.0, 1.0]$, where r is a ratio or percentage of moves available either to 'X' or to 'O' on any given turn in any given game that lead to failure. If such a ratio r exists, then we know, at least theoretically, the size of the failure database. Assume s is the theoretical size of our failure database.

$$s = 9r \binom{9}{0} \binom{9}{0} + 8r \binom{9}{1} \binom{8}{0} + 7r \binom{9}{1} \binom{8}{1} + 6r \binom{9}{2} \binom{7}{1} +$$

$$5r \binom{9}{2} \binom{7}{2} + 4r \binom{9}{3} \binom{6}{2} + 3r \binom{9}{3} \binom{6}{3} + 2r \binom{9}{4} \binom{5}{3} +$$

$$r \binom{9}{4} \binom{5}{4} = 19,107r$$

The maximum value of s occurs when $r = 1.0$. Call this maximum value s_{max}. Obviously, $s_{max} = 19,107$. In practice, and in our implementation, we know the experimental value of s, called s_{exp}, , and we can solve the above equation for the experimental value of r, r_{exp}.

$$r_{exp} = \frac{s_{exp}}{s_{max}}$$

Our experimental results are reported later, including the experimental values of s_{exp}. From these experimental results, we compute a value for r_{exp} for the game of tic-tac-toe, assuming the ratio r exists.

So, theoretically, in the worst case, for the game of tic-tac-toe, the failure database will be no larger than $19,107$. In this worst case, all possible moves for either 'X' or 'O' on any given turn in any given game lead to failure. This is a logical impossibility, since in any single completed game of tic-tac-toe, 'X' and 'O' can't both lose in the same game. Just think of $19,107$ as an upper-bound on the size of our failure database, s, in the game of tic-tac-toe. The actual size of the failure database is less than half its maximum size, and we report these results later.

5 Results

Our system was tested four times, each time starting with a null or empty failure database. In order, the system played 1,000 games, 10,000 games, 100,000 games, and 1,000,000 games of tic-tac-toe. Figure 1 shows, in table format, some of the recorded statistics for each of the four tests. Figure 2 shows the number of tie-games, X-victories, and O-victories as a function of the number of games played. Figure 2 is plotted on a logarithmic versus logarithmic scale, so all the data is visible.

It is obvious that our system learns how to play tic-tac-toe, or at least, it learns how not to lose. Notice that the statistics for X-victories and O-victories are the same when the system played either 100,000 games or 1,000,000 games, except for the number of failures avoided, since a different number of games

Games	1,000	10,000	100,000	1,000,000
tie-games	138	4,493	93,787	993,787
X-victories	558	3,350	3,824	3,824
O-victories	304	2,157	2,389	2,389
failures avoided	705	76,570	1,571,823	16,635,566

Figure 1: Performance

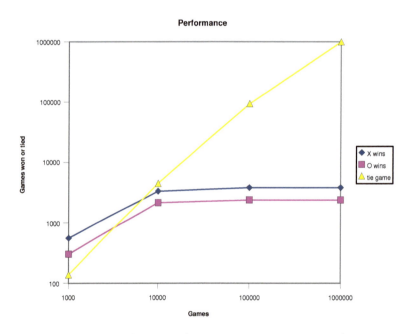

Figure 2: Performance (logarithmic vs. logarithmic)

were played in each case. When either 100,000 or 1,000,000 games were played, the usual result was a tie-game, and a huge number of failures were avoided in both cases. I cannot claim that there are only 3,824 unique X-victories in the game of tic-tac-toe, and I also cannot claim that there are only 2,389 unique O-victories in the game of tic-tac-toe, since our system chooses moves randomly, using a random number generator which I will not describe. Since the choice of moves is random, we cannot support either claim.

Figure 3 shows, in table format, the size of the failure database at the end of each experiment. Figure 4 plots the data from Figure 3. The failure database grows quickly and stabilizes.

Games	1,000	10,000	100,000	1,000,000
Size of failure database	862	5,656	6,409	6,409

Figure 3: s experimental

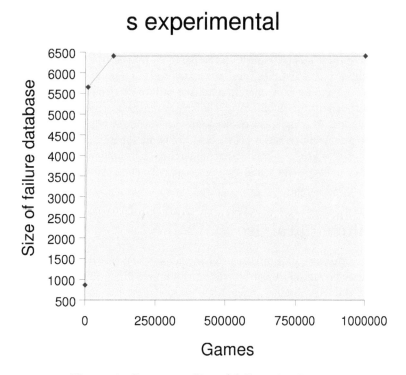

Figure 4: Games vs. Size of failure database

After playing 1,000,000 games, the failure database contains 6,409 unique failures. Again, even though the size of the failure database is the same when either 100,000 games or 1,000,000 games were played, I cannot claim that the failure database of size 6,409 includes all possible and unique failures in the game of tic-tac-toe. Again, since moves are chosen randomly using a random number generator which I will not describe, the claim cannot be supported.

Remember, s_{exp} is our best estimate of the size of the failure database after our best experiment, so $s_{exp} = 6,409$. From s_{exp} we can compute the ratio r_{exp}, assuming the ratio r exists. Using the formula from the theory section, and using $s_{exp} = 6,409$, we find that $r_{exp} = .3354$ or $r_{exp} = 33.54\%$. In other words, if the ratio r exists, then whether it is X's turn to play, or O's turn to play, 33.54% of the legal moves available to 'X' or to 'O' on any given turn of any given game of tic-tac-toe, will result in a failure or loss of the game.

6 Summary

The methodology we employ in the domain of tic-tac-toe is generally applicable to many, if not all, domains of interest to researchers in artificial intelligence, and not just generally applicable to some, but not all, of the domains of games. Applications in every domain of interest to researchers in artificial intelligence have choices. Some of these choices lead to failure, however failure is defined. Whether the choices made are optimal or not, intelligent software should avoid making choices which lead to failure. One way to avoid failure is to not repeat the same or similar mistake made in the past. A database, however represented, can store these past mistakes, and the database can be accessed by intelligent software to determine if a current choice available to the intelligent software might lead to a failure. In this way, choices available to the intelligent software can be excluded, leaving only choices which, we hope, will not lead to failure because the given choice is not represented in some form in the failure database. After this process is completed, another artificial intelligence system can then make a choice between the remaining options, with the options leading to failure, hopefully, already removed.

A Failure database

The failure database, as implemented in our system, is a simple text file. For the purposes of example, Figure 5 shows the first three failures from the failure database in the experiment where 1,000 games of tic-tac-toe were played.

The first line of the failure database specifies the number of failures in the failure database. Then for each failure in the failure database, a unique tic-tac-toe board is specified along with the coordinates of the move which lead to failure in the specified tic-tac-toe board, (y, x). The coordinates are in $(row, column)$ format, where $y, x \in \{0, 1, 2\}$. A unique tic-tac-toe board is specified first by the player, 'X' or 'O,' whose turn it is to move, and then by the tic-tac-toe board itself. The entire file or failure database, in our implementation, is a plain text file.

```
862 failures
O to play
 X      O
 X  X   O
 O  X
(0, 1)
O to play
 X
 X  O
    O  X
(0, 2)
X to play
    X  X

    O  O
(1,1)
```

Figure 5: Sample failure database

II. A new compression and decompression algorithm for files and packets

A new compression and decompression algorithm for files and packets

James A. Riechel

November 30, 2007

Abstract

A new algorithm for compressing and decompressing data is presented which is not computationally expensive, produces interesting partially encoded and non-encoded output, performs well on all types and different types of input, and which might be appropriate for the compression and decompression of files, as well as packets traveling across a network. The algorithm requires computation on the order of $O(n)$, where n specifies the linear size of the input. We make a logical argument that the time complexity of both algorithms is $O(n)$, and empirical evidence supports running times of $O(n)$ for both the compression and the decompression algorithms. We consider the case of compressing and decompressing completely random data, using a random number generator which we will not describe. Both the compression and decompression algorithms require $O(n)$ time to compress and to decompress completely random data, and the output of the compression algorithm is not much larger than the completely random input.

1 Compression algorithm

The compression algorithm presented in this article is effective and is based a simple concept, even if its expression in algorithmic form is complex. Each character or byte in the input character or byte stream is directly encoded without change or modification in the compressed output stream. Then, if the given character or byte reappears or reoccurs in the next 2,040 characters or bytes, skipping characters or bytes that have already been encoded as reappearances or recurrences of previous bytes or characters, these reappearances or recurrences are encoded if the choice to encode the reappearances or recurrences saves space in the compressed output stream. Otherwise, no encoding is performed, and the next character or byte in the input character or byte stream is encoded without change or modification, and its reappearances or recurrences are possibly encoded if the choice to encode saves space, etc.

Consider the input character or byte stream 'ABAB'. The first character or byte in this input character or byte stream is 'A'. Another 'A' reappears or reoccurs within the next 2,040 bytes or characters. In fact, it appears two characters later. This second occurrences of 'A' is not encoded because doing so will not save space. If we chose to encode the second appearance or occurrence of 'A', first we'd encode the first 'A' without change or modification, followed by the escape sequences, 00000000_2. The escape sequence indicates to the decompression algorithm that an encoding follows. If a natural 00000000_2 occurs in the input character or byte stream, 00000000_2 is encoded twice in the output stream to indicate that the $00000000_2\ 00000000_2$ should not be interpreted as an encoding, but as a natural occurrence of 00000000_2. Next, following the escape sequence, a byte or character is used to specify the length of the encoding in bytes, which can be any number between 1 and 255. The encoding itself then follows the length of the encoding, which was preceded by the escape sequence.

In our example where our input character or byte stream is 'ABAB', and assuming we chose to encode the second appearance or occurrence of 'A' even though it doesn't save space, the encoding length would be 1 byte or character, and the encoding itself would be 010. But bits are represented in groups of 8 as bytes. So, appending 0's, the encoding would be 01000000. The left-most 0 in this encoding indicates that the character immediately following the first 'A' is not a reappearance or recurrences of 'A'. In fact, it's a 'B', not an 'A'. The 1 that then follows indicates that the character following 'B' is the first and only reappearance or recurrence of 'A' in the input character or byte stream.

Let's continue with this example, where our input character or byte stream is 'ABAB'. Assume we encoded the first and second appearance or occurrence of 'A', and we are now considering the first appearance or occurrence of 'B'. Assume also that even though it will not save space, we choose to encode all reappearances or recurrences of 'B' after the first 'B'. So, first 'B' would be encoded without modification or change in the output stream, followed by the escape sequence, 00000000_2, followed by the length of the stream, again 1, followed by the encoding. The encoding itself skips the 'A' that follows the first 'B' since this 'A' was encoded as a reappearance or recurrence after the first 'A'. So, our encoded sequence is simply 1. But bits are represented in groups of eight (8) as bytes, so appending 0's we get 10000000. The left-most one (1) encodes the second 'B' in our input byte or character stream.

A more complicated compression example is given in Appendix A.

When deciding whether or not to encode reappearances or recurrences of a character or byte in our input stream, we look at the following 2,040 characters or bytes in the input stream that have not already been encoded as reappearances or recurrences of a previous character or byte in the input stream. If we choose to encode, after the escape sequence, we specify the length of the encoding measured in bytes, a number between 1 and 255. The number zero (0) is reserved for the escape sequence, and if the number zero appears twice in-a-row, it specifies a natural 0 (zero) in our input stream. Notice that $255 * 8 = 2,040$. We look no father than 2,040 bytes or characters ahead, because an encoding of length 255, measures in bytes, represents 2,040 bits.

Figures 1 and 2 specify the compression algorithm. Figure 2 is the algorithm for COMPRESS, which uses the helper function ENCODE. Figure 1 is the algorithm for ENCODE. Parameters passed to either function, either COMPRESS or ENCODE, which are preceded by **var** are passed by reference, so their values can change in the algorithms.

ENCODE (*uncompressed_data, i, claimed,* **var** *newly_claimed,* **var** *encoded,* **var** *length_stream*)

1	$byte\_index \leftarrow 0$
2	$bit\_index \leftarrow 0$
3	$j \leftarrow i + 1$
4	$skipped \leftarrow 0$
5	$encoded \leftarrow 0$
6	$stream[0] \leftarrow 00000000_2$
7	**while** $j - i \leq 2040$ **and** $j + skipped < length(uncompressed\_data)$ **do**
8	**if** not $claimed[j + skipped]$ **then**
9	**if** $uncompressed\_data[j + skipped] = uncompressed\_data[i]$ **then**
10	Set 2^{bit_index} bit of $stream[byte\_index]$ to binary 1
11	$newly\_claimed[j + skipped] \leftarrow true$
12	$encoded \leftarrow encoded + 1$
13	**else** Set 2^{bit_index} bit of $stream[byte\_index]$ to binary 0
14	$bit\_index \leftarrow bit\_index + 1$
15	**if** $bit\_index > 7$ **then**
16	$bit\_index \leftarrow 0$
17	$byte\_index \leftarrow byte\_index + 1$
18	$stream[byte\_index] \leftarrow 00000000_2$
19	$j \leftarrow j + 1$
20	**else** $skipped \leftarrow skipped + 1$
21	**while** $byte\_index \geq 0$ **and** $stream[byte\_index] = 00000000_2$ **do**
22	$byte\_index \leftarrow byte\_index - 1$
23	$length\_stream \leftarrow byte\_index + 1$
24	**return** $stream$

Figure 1: ENCODE

2 Decompression algorithm

Let's consider decompressing the example given in the previous section. In the previous section we considered compressing the character or byte stream 'ABAB'. Assume we chose to encode the second and only reappearances or recurrences of both 'A' and 'B', even though it does not save space. Given this assumption, from the previous section, 'ABAB' is compressed as:

COMPRESS (*uncompressed_data*, **var** *length_compressed_data*)

1	*length_compressed_data* ← 0
2	**for** i ← 0 **to** *length*(*uncompressed_data*) – 1 **do**
3	*claimed*[i] ← *false*
4	**for** i ← 0 **to** *length*(*uncompressed_data*) – 1 **do**
5	**if** not *claimed*[i] **then**
6	*claimed*[i] ← *true*
7	*compressed_data*[*length_compressed_data*] ← *uncompressed_data*[i]
8	*length_compressed_data* ← *length_compressed_data* + 1
9	**if** *uncompressed_data*[i] = 00000000_2 **then**
10	*compressed_data*[*length_compressed_data*] ← 00000000_2
11	*length_compressed_data* ← *length_compressed_data* + 1
12	*count* ← 0
13	j ← i + 1
14	**while** *count* < 2040 **and** j < *length*(*uncompressed_data*) **do**
15	**if** not *claimed*[j] **then**
16	*count* ← *count* + 1
17	*newly_claimed*[j] ← *false*
18	j ← j + 1
19	*encoded* ← 0
20	*length_stream* ← 0
21	*stream* ← ENCODE (*uncompressed_data*, i, *claimed*, *newly_claimed*, *encoded*,*length_stream*)
22	**if** (*length_stream* + 2) < *encoded* **then**
23	*compressed_data*[*length_compressed_data*] ← 00000000_2
24	*length_compressed_data* ← *length_compressed_data* + 1
25	*compressed_data*[*length_compressed_data*] ← *length_stream*
26	*length_compressed_data* ← *length_compressed_data* + 1
27	**for** j ← 0 **to** *length_stream* – 1 **do**
28	*compressed_data*[*length_compressed_data*] ← *stream*[j]
29	*length_compressed_data* ← *length_compressed_data* + 1
30	*count* ← 0
31	j ← i + 1
32	**while** *count* < 2040 **and** j < *length*(*uncompressed_data*) **do**
33	**if** not *claimed*[j] **then**
34	*count* ← *count* + 1
35	*claimed*[j] ← *claimed*[j] ∨ *newly_claimed*[j]
36	j ← j + 1
37	**return** *compressed_data*

Figure 2: COMPRESS

A 00000000 00000001 01000000 B 00000000 00000001 10000000

This is our compressed input stream, and we will form a decompressed output stream. The 'A' is immediately read and placed into the decompressed output stream. Then 00000000_2 follows. This is the escape sequence, so we know an encoding follows, which encodes the reappearances or recurrences of 'A'. If another escape sequence, 00000000_2, followed the first escape sequence, it would really specify a natural 00000000_2 in the compressed input stream, and we would not assume that an encoding followed. Next is 00000001_2. This is the length of the encoding measured in bytes, namely 1 (one). Then the encoding itself follows, 01000000_2, an encoding of length one (1), measured in bytes. This encoding indicates that not the next character, but the character after the next charter is a reappearance or recurrence of 'A'. So this is our decompressed output stream so far: 'A?A?', where question marks (?'s) represent currently missing or unknown information.

Next we read 'B' from the compressed input stream. This is immediately placed in the decompressed output stream, so our decompressed output stream is currently 'ABA?'. Then the escape sequence, 00000000_2, follows, so we know an encoding follows, an encoding which encodes reappearances or recurrences of 'B'. Next is 00000001_2. This is the length of the encoding measured in bytes, namely 1 (one). Then the encoding itself follows, 10000000_2, an encoding of length one (1), measured in bytes. This encoding indicates the next question mark (?) in our decompressed output stream is a reappearance or recurrence of 'B'. So that completes our decompressed output stream: 'ABAB'. We have decompressed the compressed version of 'ABAB'.

A more complicated decompression example is given in Appendix B.

Figures 3 and 4 specify the decompression algorithm. Figure 4 is the algorithm for DECOMPRESS, which uses the helper function DECODE. Figure 3 is the algorithm for DECODE. Parameters passed to either function, either DECOMPRESS or DECODE, which are preceded by **var** are passed by reference, so their values can change in the algorithms.

3 Time complexity

Both the compression and decompression algorithms require time on the order of $O(n)$, where n specifies the linear size of the input. In other words, both algorithms are linear, and can compress and decompress data quickly.

3.1 Time complexity of the compression algorithm

As previously mentioned, the compression algorithm is linear with respect to the size of the input. COMPRESS requires the helper function ENCODE. Let's look at ENCODE first.

DECODE (*compressed_data*, **var** *i*, **var** *uncompressed_data*, **var** *j*, **var** *claimed*)

1	*character* ← *compressed_data*[*i*]
2	*uncompressed_data*[*j*] ← *character*
3	*claimed*[*j*] ← *true*
4	**while** *j* < *length*(*uncompressed_data*) **and** *claimed*[*j*] **do**
5	*j* ← *j* + 1
6	*i* ← *i* + 1
7	**if** *compressed_data*[*i* − 1] = 00000000$_2$ **and** *compressed_data*[*i*] = 00000000$_2$ **then**
8	*i* ← *i* + 1
9	**if** *i* < *length*(*compressed_data*) **then**
10	**if** *compressed_data*[*i*] = 00000000$_2$ **and** *compressed_data*[*i* + 1] ≠ 00000000$_2$ **then**
11	*count* ← 0
12	*k* ← *j*
13	**while** *count* < 2040 **and** *k* < *length*(*uncompressed_data*) **do**
14	**if not** *claimed*[*k*] **then**
15	*count* ← *count* + 1
16	*newly_claimed*[*k*] ← *false*
17	*k* ← *k* + 1
18	*i* ← *i* + 1
19	*encoding_length* ← *compressed_data*[*i*]
20	*j*$_2$ ← *j*
21	**for** *k* = 0 **to** *encoding_length* − 1 **do**
22	*i* ← *i* + 1
23	*encoded_byte* ← *compressed_data*[*i*]
24	**for** *l* = 0 **to** 7 **do**
25	**if** 2^l bit of *encoded_byte* set to binary 1 **then**
26	*uncompressed_data*[*j*$_2$] ← *character*
27	*newly_claimed*[*j*$_2$] ← *true*
28	*j*$_2$ ← *j*$_2$ + 1
29	**while** *j*$_2$ < *length*(*uncompressed_data*) **and** *claimed*[*j*$_2$] **do**
30	*j*$_2$ ← *j*$_2$ + 1
31	*i* ← *i* + 1
32	*count* ← 0
33	*k* ← *j*
34	**while** *count* < 2040 **and** *k* < *length*(*uncompressed_data*) **do**
35	**if** *claimed*[*k*] **then**
36	*count* ← *count* + 1
37	*claimed*[*k*] ← *claimed*[*k*] ∨ *newly_claimed*[*k*]
38	*k* ← *k* + 1

Figure 3: DECODE

1	**for** $i \leftarrow 0$ **to** *length_uncompressed_data* – 1 **do**
2	*claimed*[*i*] $\leftarrow$ *false*
3	$i \leftarrow 0$
4	$j \leftarrow 0$
5	**while** i < *length*(*compressed_data*) **do**
6	DECODE (*compressed_data, i, uncompressed_data, j, claimed*)
7	**while** j < *length_uncompressed_data* **and** *claimed*[*j*] **do**
8	$j \leftarrow j + 1$
9	**return** *uncompressed_data*

Figure 4: DECOMPRESS

ENCODE has two loop structures: the while loop at line 7, and the while loop at line 21. There are no other loop constructs in ENCODE. Both while loops do a constant amount of work, so the function ENCODE itself does a constant amount of work. Let's now examine COMPRESS.

In COMPRESS, the for loops at lines 2 and 4 do a linear amount of work, or $O(n)$ work. The while loop at line 14, the for loop at line 27, and the while loop at line 32, all do a constant amount of work. COMPRESS calls ENCODE on line 21, but remember ENCODE itself does a constant amount of work. Therefore, COMPRESS is linear or does a linear amount of work to compress input data. If n is the linear size of the input, COMPRESS requires time on the order of $O(n)$ to compress input data.

Figure 5 plots the time it takes to generate random data, and then compress it. The open circles in the plot represent real data to which the plotted line was fit. If the x-axis or the size of the input is n, and if the y-axis or time measured in seconds is t, then the equation of the line fitted to the real data is approximately:

$$t = 0.000077059n + 0.3867179$$

In other words, in the generation and compression of random data, the compression algorithm has overhead of approximately 0.3867179 seconds, and it takes approximately 0.00007705963 seconds to compress each byte in the random data.

3.2 Time complexity of the decompression algorithm

As previously mentioned, the decompression algorithm is linear with respect to the size of the input. DECOMPRESS requires the helper function DECODE. Let's look at DECODE first.

DECODE has six loop constructs: the while loop on line 4, the while loop on line 13, the for loop on line 21, the for loop on line 24, the while loop on line

Compression Times (Random Data)

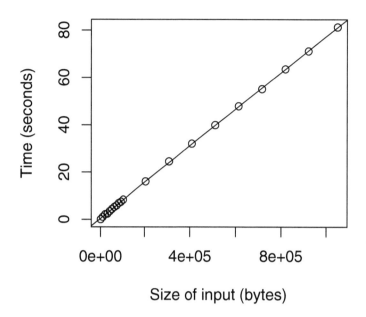

Figure 5: Size of input vs. Time (Random Data)

29, and the while loop on line 34. All six of these loop constructs do a constant amount of work. Therefore, the function DECODE itself does a constant amount of work. Let's now examine DECOMPRESS.

In DECOMPRESS, the for loop on line 1, and the while loop on line 5, both do a linear amount of work, or $O(n)$ work. The while loop on line 7 does a constant amount of work. DECOMPRESS calls DECODE on line 6, but remember DECODE itself does a constant amount of work. Therefore, DECOMPRESS is linear or does a linear amount of work to decompress input data. If n is the linear size of the input, DECOMPRESS requires time on the order of $O(n)$ to decompress input data.

Figure 6 plots the time it takes to generate random data, and then decompress it. The open circles in the plot represent real data to which the plotted line was fit. If the x-axis or the size of the input is n, and if the y-axis or time measured in seconds is t, then the equation of the line fitted to the real data is approximately:

$$t = 0.0000006301167n + 0.01284272$$

In other words, in the generation and decompression of random data, the decompression algorithm has overhead of approximately 0.01284272 seconds, and it takes approximately 0.0000006301167 seconds to decompress each byte in the random data.

Decompression Times (Random Data)

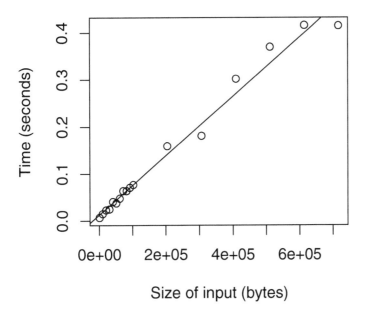

Figure 6: Size of input vs. Time (Random Data)

A   Compression example

Consider the following character or byte stream, which we wish to compress.

```
Alan Alan Alan Alan Alan Alan Alan Alan Alan
```

There are 44 characters or bytes in this character or byte stream, and we wish to compress it, so it uses less memory. The first character in the character or byte stream is 'A'. This is immediately encoded into the compressed output stream. It is obvious, but this is our compressed output stream so far:

```
A
```

After this first 'A', additional A's occur 5 characters or bytes later, 10 characters or bytes later, 15 characters or bytes later, 20 characters or bytes later, 25 characters or bytes later, 30 characters or bytes later, 35 characters or bytes later, and 40 characters or bytes later. That's the other eight A's occurring in the character or byte stream. Each 'Alan' begins with a capital 'A', and there are eight Alan's following the first 'Alan'.

For each of the forty-three (43) characters following the first 'A', we can assign a binary digit. This binary digit is equal to zero (0_2) if the character is not an 'A', and is equal to one (1_2) if the character is equal to 'A'. Let's look at this stream of binary digits:

```
00001000 01000010 00010000 10000100 00100001 000
```

Next, there are three (3) zeros at the tail of this binary stream. But in any implementation, binary digits are represented as bytes, which are eight bits a piece. So, it our representation, this bit steam is actually:

```
00001000 01000010 00010000 10000100 00100001 00000000
```

So, this is the binary encoding of the forty-three (43) characters that follow the first 'A', represented as six (6) bytes. Next, we strip away trailing 00000000's from the bit or byte stream. These trailing 00000000's are unnecessary, and waste space should we choose to encode them later. So, our binary or byte stream is now:

```
00001000 01000010 00010000 10000100 00100001
```

It will take 5 characters or bytes of space to encode or represent these eight additional occurrences of 'A' following the first 'A'. But we also need to encode the escape sequence, 00000000_2, following the 'A' which we have already encoded, and after the escape sequence we need to specify the number of bytes or characters in the encoded byte stream, namely five (5). The number 5 in binary is 00000101_2. So, it takes $1 + 1 + 5 = 7$ characters to represent these eight additional A's. Since $7 < 8$, the algorithm chooses to encode in this format, to save space. So, here's our compressed output so far:

```
A 0000000 00000101 00001000 01000010 00010000 10000100
0010000100
```

The next unique character in our input is 'l'. It is immediately encoded:

```
A 0000000 00000101 00001000 01000010 00010000 10000100
00100001 l
```

Once again, there are eight more occurrences of 'l', but this time we skip all the additional A's previously encoded. Ignoring these already encoded A's, after the first 'l', l's occur 4 characters or bytes later, 8 characters or bytes later, 12 characters or bytes later, 16 characters or bytes later, 20 characters or bytes later, 24 characters or bytes later, 28 characters or bytes later, and 32 characters or bytes later. As before, here is how these recurrences are represented as a binary stream of digits:

```
00010001 00010001 00010001 00010001 00
```

There are forty-two (42) binary digits in this bit stream, but, again, in any implementation, bits are represented as bytes, so we append additional 0's to create five (5) bytes:

```
00010001 00010001 00010001 00010001 00000000
```

But again, the last byte, 00000000_2, encodes nothing, and would only waste space if we chose to encode it. Therefore, it is removed from the encoding. This leaves us with the following bit or byte stream:

00010001 00010001 00010001 00010001

Each of these binary numbers take one character or byte to represent in compressed format. But once again, after the 'l' we need to include the escape sequence, 00000000_2, and the number of bytes in the bit or byte stream, namely four (4) or 00000100_2. So a total of 6 bytes is required to represent these additional eight occurrences of 'l'. Since $6 < 8$, the encoded representation is chosen. So, here's our compressed output:

A 00000000 00000101 00001000 01000010 00010000 10000100
00100001 l 00000000 00000100 00010001 00010001 00010001
00010001

The next unique character in our input is 'a'. It is immediately encoded:

A 00000000 00000101 00001000 01000010 00010000 10000100
00100001 l 00000000 00000100 00010001 00010001 00010001
00010001 a

Now eight additional a's occur in the input. We ignore already encoded characters, namely, the last eight A's and the last eight l's. Ignoring these already encoded letters, after the first 'a', additional a's occur 3 characters or bytes later, 6 characters or bytes later, 9 characters or bytes later, 12 characters or bytes later, 15 characters or bytes later, 18 characters or bytes later, 21 characters or bytes later, and 24 characters or bytes later. Again, these recurrences are represented as a binary stream of digits:

00100100 10010010 01001001 0

But once again, in any implementation, bits are represented as bytes, so the tailing zero (0) is really represented by 8-bits, with zero's (0's) appended, or:

00100100 10010010 01001001 00000000

But once again, the tailing byte, 00000000_2, encodes nothing, and would waste space if we chose to encode it, so it is trimmed from the binary bit or byte stream, leaving:

00100100 10010010 01001001

Once again, these three bytes or characters must be precede by the escape sequence, 00000000_2, and the number of bytes in the stream, namely three (3) or 00000011_2. Therefore, $1 + 1 + 3 = 5$ characters are necessary to represent the eight additional l's. Since $5 < 8$, we choose to encode the eight additional a's in this manner, so now the compress output looks like:

```
A 00000000 00000101 00001000 01000010 00010000 10000100
00100001 l 00000000 00000100 00010001 00010001 00010001
00010001 a 00000000 00000011 00100100 10010010 01001001
```

The next unique character in our input is 'n'. It is immediately represented in our output:

```
A 00000000 00000101 00001000 01000010 00010000 10000100
00100001 l 00000000 00000100 00010001 00010001 00010001
00010001 a 00000000 00000011 00100100 10010010 01001001
n
```

After this first occurrence of 'n', there are eight additional occurrences of 'n'. Ignoring the characters that have already been encoded, 'A', 'l', and 'a', after the first 'n', n's occur after 2 characters or bytes, 4 characters or bytes, 6 characters or bytes, 8 characters or bytes, 10 characters or bytes, 12 characters or bytes, 14 characters or bytes, and 16 characters or bytes. These recurrences are represented as:

```
01010101 01010101
```

These two binary numbers are each represented by a single character or byte, but we must also include the escape sequence, 00000000_2, and the number of characters or bytes in the stream, namely two (2), or 00000010_2. Therefore, $1 + 1 + 2 = 4$ characters or bytes are needed to represent these additional eight occurrences of 'n'. Since, $4 < 8$ we choose to encode. Our output is now:

```
A 00000000 00000101 00001000 01000010 00010000 10000100
00100001 l 00000000 00000100 00010001 00010001 00010001
00010001 a 00000000 00000011 00100100 10010010 01001001
n 00000000 00000010 01010101 01010101
```

The next unique character in our input is the space character, ' '. It is immediately represented in our output:

```
A 00000000 00000101 00001000 01000010 00010000 10000100
00100001 l 00000000 00000100 00010001 00010001 00010001
00010001 a 00000000 00000011 00100100 10010010 01001001
n 00000000 00000010 01010101 01010101 ' '
```

After this first space, ' ', seven additional spaces occur. Ignoring characters that have already been encoded, 'A', 'l', 'a', and 'n', after the first space, ' ', additional spaces occur after 1 character or byte, 2 characters or bytes, 3 characters or bytes, 4 characters or bytes, 5 characters or bytes, 6 characters or bytes, and 7 characters or bytes. This can be represented as:

```
1111111
```

But in any implementation, bits are represented in groups of 8 as bytes, so we need to add a single zero (0) to the end of this stream to make it a full byte:

```
11111110
```

This binary number will be represented as a single character or byte in the output. As usual, we'll also have to include the escape sequence, 00000000_2, after the first space, and the number of bytes in the binary bit or byte stream, namely one (1), or 00000001_2. So, it'll take $1 + 1 + 1 = 3$ characters or bytes to represent these additional seven spaces, ' '. Since $3 < 7$, we encode in this fashion. Here's our output:

```
A 00000000 00000101 00001000 01000010 00010000 10000100
00100001 1 00000000 00000100 00010001 00010001 00010001
00010001 a 00000000 00000011 00100100 10010010 01001001
n 00000000 00000010 01010101 01010101 ' ' 00000000 00000001
11111110
```

Now the entire input character or byte stream has been compressed or encoded. Remember, the input character or byte stream was 44 characters or bytes in length. In comparison, the compressed output is only 30 characters of bytes in length. Compression has been successful.

B Decompression example

Let's take the compressed output from the example in Appendix A, and decompress it. Remember, the compressed output from this example looked like:

```
A 00000000 00000101 00001000 01000010 00010000 10000100
00100001 1 00000000 00000100 00010001 00010001 00010001
00010001 a 00000000 00000011 00100100 10010010 01001001
n 00000000 00000010 01010101 01010101 ' ' 00000000 00000001
11111110
```

The non-encoded 'A' is read and placed in our decompressed output. Here's our decompressed output so far. Periods, '.', represent empty or unassigned spaces or characters. Note that we assume we know the size of the decompressed output before we decompress the input.

```
A.......................................
```

Next, the escape sequences follows, 00000000_2, and then the length of the encoded sequence measured in bytes is given, 00000101_2, or five (5). The five bytes that then follow specify additional occurrences of 'A' in our decompressed output. We decode these, giving:

```
A....A....A....A....A....A....A....A....A...
```

Next, an 'l' occurs, and this is immediately added to the decompressed output:

```
Al...A....A....A....A....A....A....A....A...
```

After the 'l', the escape sequence occurs, 00000000_2, followed by the number of bytes in the encoded sequence, 00000100_2, or four (4). The four bytes that then follow specify additional occurrences of 'l' in our decompressed output. We decode these, giving:

```
Al...Al...Al...Al...Al...Al...Al...Al...Al..
```

Next, an 'a' occurs, and this is immediately added to our decompressed output:

```
Ala..Al...Al...Al...Al...Al...Al...Al...Al..
```

The escape sequence, 00000000_2, then follows the 'a', and after the escape sequence, the number of bytes in the encoding is given, 00000011_2, or three (3). The three bytes that then follow specify additional occurrences of 'a' in the decompressed output. We decode these, giving:

```
Ala..Ala..Ala..Ala..Ala..Ala..Ala..Ala..Ala.
```

Next, an 'n' occurs, and this is immediately added to our decompressed output:

```
Alan.Ala..Ala..Ala..Ala..Ala..Ala..Ala..Ala.
```

The escape sequence, 00000000_2, follows the 'n', and after the escape sequence, the number of bytes in the encoding is given, 00000010_2, or two (2). The two bytes that then follow specify additional occurrences of 'n' in the decompressed output. We decode these, giving:

```
Alan.Alan.Alan.Alan.Alan.Alan.Alan.Alan.Alan
```

Next, a space, or ' ', occurs, and this is immediately added to our decompressed output:

```
Alan Alan.Alan.Alan.Alan.Alan.Alan.Alan.Alan
```

The escape sequence, 00000000_2, follows the space, and after the escape sequence, the number of bytes in the encoding is given, 00000001_2, or one (1). The one byte that then follows specifies additional occurrences of the space, or ' ', in the decompressed output. We decode these, giving:

```
Alan Alan Alan Alan Alan Alan Alan Alan Alan
```

We have decompressed the compressed output from Appendix A.

III. A simple load-balancing protocol for min-max depth-first search

A simple load-balancing protocol for min-max depth-first search

James A. Riechel*

December 16, 2007

Abstract

We load-balance min-max depth-first search in a simulated parallel and distributed environment using a simple broadcast and share-half-my-work protocol. We choose a rich sub-domain of chess to search in, where en passant capture is not allowed, where neither king can castle king-side or queen-side, where the kings can be captured but are too valuable to lose, and where pawns do not and cannot promote. Four experiments are performed on two different platforms. The four experiments on both platforms use a different number of nodes or processes. These nodes or processes cooperate together to accomplish a common search task. In order, 1 node or process is used, 10 nodes or processes are used, 100 nodes or processes are used, and 1,000 nodes or processes are used, on both platforms. When an experiment is complete, each node or process reports the virtual time of its execution in virtual seconds. Each evaluation of a chess position counts as one virtual second ($1s$). A simple wood-count evaluation function is used. Time series data, the virtual time each node or process takes in each experiment on both platforms, is reported and analyzed to determine how well the simple broadcast and share-half-my-work protocol balances the load across all nodes or processes in each experiment on both platforms. Efficiency, and other metrics of performance, are computed and presented.

---

*jamesriechel@gmail.com

IV. A recursive binary search algorithm for partially sorted data

A recursive binary search algorithm for partially sorted data

James A. Riechel

January 20, 2009

Abstract

A recursive binary search algorithm is presented which is appropriate for searching partially sorted data. In the case of completely random input, the algorithm requires on the average of $O(an + b\lg n + c)$ operations to find a specified key in a list of length n. In the case of partially sorted data, on average $O(an + b\lg n + c)$ operations are also required to find a specified key in a list of length n. In the case of completely sorted data, on average only $O(a\lg n + b)$ operations are necessary to find a specified key in a list of length n, assuming the specified search key can be found in our list, the same average case running time as ordinary binary search on completely sorted data.

1 Algorithm

To recursively search for a specified key, *key*, in a list of length n, $data[0], ..., data[n-1]$, a call to $rbspsd(data, key, 0, n-1)$ is made. The author considers the recursive binary search algorithm for partially sorted data, $rbspsd()$, to be classified, but the C or C++ code for $rbspsd()$ can be found in Figure 1.

```
int rbspsd(int* data, int key, int n1, int n2) {

    if (n2 < n1) return -1;

    int m = ((int) ((n2 - n1 + 1) / 2)) + n1;

    if (key == data[m]) return m;

    int result;

    if (key < data[m]) {
        if ((result = rbspsd(data, key, n1, m - 1)) != -1) return result;
        if ((result = rbspsd(data, key, m + 1, n2)) != -1) return result;
    }
    else { // key > data[m]
        if ((result = rbspsd(data, key, m + 1, n2)) != -1) return result;
        if ((result = rbspsd(data, key, n1, m - 1)) != -1) return result;
    }

    return -1;
}
```

Figure 1: Recursive binary search for partially sorted data, *rbspsd()*.

2 Time complexity

The time complexity of the $rbspsd()$ algorithm depends on the data distribution of the input: $data[0],...,...data[n-1]$, for a list of length n, and it depends on whether or not the specified search key can be found in our list. We consider the cases of completely random input before and after partial sorting, and the case of completely sorted input.

2.1 Completely random input

Assume the input to the algorithm is completely random data, $data[0],...,data[n-1]$, for a list of length n, and assume we are searching for a specified key, key. Now define

$$m = \left\lfloor \frac{n_2 - n_1 + 1}{2} \right\rfloor + n_1 = n_2 + 1 - \left\lceil \frac{n_2 - n_1 + 1}{2} \right\rceil$$

Since the input is completely random:

$$P(key = data[m]) = \frac{1}{n_2 - n_1 + 1}$$

$$P(key < data[m]) = \frac{\left\lfloor \frac{n_2 - n_1 + 1}{2} \right\rfloor}{n_2 - n_1 + 1}$$

$$P(key > data[m]) = \frac{\left\lceil \frac{n_2 - n_1 + 1}{2} \right\rceil - 1}{n_2 - n_1 + 1}$$

Now define $n = n_2 - n_1 + 1$. Then the running time of the algorithm, $R(n)$, is given by:

$$R(n < 1) = c$$

$$R(n \geq 1) = P(key = data[m])c_0 + P(key < data[m]) \left[c_1 R\left(\left\lceil \frac{n}{2} \right\rceil - 1 \right) + c_2 R\left(\left\lfloor \frac{n}{2} \right\rfloor \right) \right] +$$

$$P(key > data[m]) \left[c_3 R\left(\left\lceil \frac{n}{2} \right\rceil \right) \right] + c_4 R\left(\left\lfloor \frac{n}{2} \right\rfloor - 1 \right)$$

Simplifying:

$$R(n < 1) = k$$

$$R(n \geq 1) = k_0 + k_1 R\left(\left\lfloor \frac{n}{2} \right\rfloor - 1\right) + k_2 R\left(\left\lfloor \frac{n}{2} \right\rfloor\right)$$

$R(n)$ is a recursive formula which, in the worst case, is linear. In other words, in the worst case, $O(R(n)) = O(n)$ for completely random data, or when $key \notin data$, since we must examine every element in the data to compare it to the specified search key, key. On average, the time complexity for completely random data is given by $O(R(n)) = O(an + b \lg n + c)$

2.2 Completely sorted input

The beauty of recursive binary search for partially sorted data is that it has the same time complexity as regular binary search if the input to the algorithm is completely sorted data. If $R(n)$ is the running time of the recursive binary search algorithm for partially sorted data, and if the input to the algorithm is completely sorted data, and if we assume $key \in data$, then the average case running time of the algorithm is given by $O(R(n)) = O(a \lg n + b)$.

However, if $key \notin data$, then $O(R(n)) = O(n)$.

2.3 Partially sorted data

We partially sort the completely random input using the partial sorting algorithm given in my last article, "A linear time algorithm for partial sorting" (2009).

As in section 2.1, the running time of the algorithm, $R(n)$, is given by:

$$R(n < 1) = k$$

$$R(n \geq 1) = k_0 + k_1 R\left(\left\lfloor \frac{n}{2} \right\rfloor - 1\right) + k_2 R\left(\left\lfloor \frac{n}{2} \right\rfloor\right)$$

As before, in the worst case, $O(R(n)) = O(n)$, and in the average case, $O(R(n)) = O(an + b \lg n + c)$.

3 Summary / Conclusion

Figure 2 summarizes the time complexity of the recursive binary search algorithm for partially sorted data. If $key \notin data$, then regardless of whether the input is completely random, partially sorted, or completely sorted, the algorithm is linear, or requires on the order of $O(n)$ operations to complete, for a list of length n. The advantage of using the $rbspsd()$ algorithm is seen when $key \in data$, and the input is either partially sorted, or completely sorted. When $key \in data$, and the input is completely sorted, there is no difference between $rbspsd()$ and regular binary search on completely sorted data. When $key \in data$, and the input is partially sorted, the $rbspsd()$ algorithm performs well in comparison to completely random input, and the benefit of partially sorting the completely random input before searching is clear and evident.

	Input	Average case	Worst case
$key \in data$	Completely random	$O(an+b\lg n+c)$ $a>b$ or $a\gg b$	$O(n)$
	Partially sorted	$O(an+b\lg n+c)$ $b>a$ or $b\gg a$	$O(n)$
	Completely sorted	$O(a\lg n+b)$	$O(a\lg n+b)$
$key \notin data$	Completely random	$O(n)$	$O(n)$
	Partially sorted	$O(n)$	$O(n)$
	Completely sorted	$O(n)$	$O(n)$

Figure 2: Time complexity of $rbspsd()$

V. A linear time algorithm for partial sorting

A linear time algorithm for partial sorting

James A. Riechel

January 23, 2009

Abstract

A linear time algorithm for partial sorting is presented which is appropriate for partially sorting long lists where sorting is computationally prohibitive, or which is appropriate for real-time applications where sorting is impossible. In a list of length n, whether sorted, partially sorted, or not, there are on the order of $O(n^2)$ possible inversions. In the algorithm presented, the number of inversions is significantly reduced – on the order of $O(n^2)$ – but, in the general case, the number of inversions is still on the order of $O(n^2)$. However, the ratio of inversions in completely random data to inversions in partially sorted completely random data, appears constant.

1 Algorithm

The partial sorting algorithm presented consists of three functions: *classified_sort*, *classified_swap*, and *classified_merge*. All three functions are given below in C or C++ code.

1.1 *classified_sort*

To partially sort a list of length n, *data[0], ..., data[n − 1]*, a call to *classified_sort(n, data)* is made. Obviously, *classified_sort()* first calls *classified_swap()*, followed by *classified_merge()*. classified_sort(n, data) assumes n is even, $n/2$ is even, and $n/4$ is even.

```
void classified_sort(int n, int* data) {
  // assume n is even, (n / 2) is even, and (n / 4) is even.
  classified_swap(n, data);
  classified_merge(n, data);
}
```

Figure 1: *classified_sort*

1.2 *classified_swap*

The author considers the swaps performed by *classified_swap()* to be classified. To perform classified swaps on a list of length n, *data[0], ..., data[n − 1]*, a call to *classified_swap(n, data)* is made. *classified_swap(n, data)* makes on the order of $O(n)$ insertion sorts on lists of length four (*4*), which amounts to any number of swaps between zero (*0*) (on already sorted data) to *3n/4* swaps. The insertion sort algorithm can be found in any computer science textbook on algorithms. *classified_swap(n, data)* assumes *n is even, $n/2$ is even*, and *$n/4$ is even*.

```
void classified_swap(int n, int* data) {
  // assume n is even, (n / 2) is even, and (n / 4) is even
  for (int i = 0; i < (n / 4); i++) {
    int temp[4];
    temp[0] = data[i];
    temp[1] = data[n / 2 - i - 1];
    temp[2] = data[i + n / 2];
    temp[3] = data[n - i - 1];
    insertion_sort(4, temp);
    data[i] = temp[0];
    data[n / 2 - i - 1] = temp[1];
    data[i + n / 2] = temp[2];
    data[n - i - 1] = temp[3];
  }
}
```

Figure 2: *classified_swap*()

1.3 *classified_merge*

classified_merge() merges the first half of a list of length *n*, *data[0]*, ..., *data[n/2 − 1]*, with the second half of the same list, *data[n/2]*, ..., *data[n − 1]*. To do this, a call to *classified_merge(n, data)* is made. *classified_merge(n, data)* calls the standard computer science merge algorithm to merge two lists together, in this case, the first half and the second half of the same list. The merge algorithm can be found in any computer science textbook on algorithms. *classified_merge(n, data)* assumes *n* is even, and *n/2* is even.

```
void classified_merge(int n, int* data) {
  // assume n is even, and (n / 2) is even
  merge(n / 2, data, n / 2, &(data[n / 2]));
}
```

Figure 3: *classified_merge*()

2   Time complexity

The partial sorting algorithm presented is a linear time algorithm. In other words, it requires on the order of $O(n)$ operations to partially sort a list of length *n*.

2.1 *classified_swap*

classified_swap() is also a linear time algorithm. It requires on the order of $O(n)$ operations to make a call to *classified_swap(n, data)*. There are *n/4* iterations of the for loop in *classified_swap*(). Inside the for loop, a constant, or $O(1)$, amount of work is done. Note that insertion sort on a list of length four (*4*) does a constant amount of work, since insertion sort is an $O(n^2)$ algorithm, and for *n = 4*, the amount of work done is $O(n^2) = O(4^2) = O(16) = O(1)$. Therefore, as mentioned before, *classified_swap(n, data)* is a linear time algorithm which requires on the order of $O(n)$ operations to complete.

2.2 *classified_merge*

classified_merge(n, data) is a linear time algorithm which requires on the order of $O(n)$ operations to complete. *classified_merge(n, data)* calls *merge(n/2, data, n/2, &(data[n/2]))*, merge being the standard computer science merge algorithm, which is also a linear time algorithm requiring on the order of $O(n)$ operations to complete. Therefore, *classified_merge(n, data)* is a linear time algorithm requiring on the order of $O(n)$ operations to complete.

2.3 *classified_sort*

classified_sort(n, data) calls *classified_swap(n, data)*, and *classified_merge(n, data)*. Both *classified_swap(n, data)*, and *classified_merge(n, data)* do a linear amount of work, or require on the order of $O(n)$ operations to complete. Therefore, *classified_sort(n, data)* requires a linear amount of time to complete, or on the order of $O(n)$ operations to complete.

3 Special cases

There are two special cases that should be mentioned.

3.1 Already sorted data

If the partial sorting algorithm is given a list which is already sorted, the partial sorting algorithm maintains the sorted order. For example, if *data[0], ..., data[n − 1]* is:

1, 2, 3, 4, 5, 6, 7, 8, 9, 10, 11, 12

the partial sorting algorithm maintains the sorted order, and the output of the algorithm, or *data[0], ..., data[n − 1]* is:

1, 2, 3, 4, 5, 6, 7, 8, 9, 10, 11, 12

3.2 Reverse sorted data

If the partial sorting algorithm is given a list in reverse sorted order, the partial sorting algorithm completely sorts the list! For example, if *data[0], ..., data[n−1]* is:

12, 11, 10, 9, 8, 7, 6, 5, 4, 3, 2, 1

the partial sorting algorithm completely sorts the list, and the output of the algorithm, or *data[0], ..., data[n − 1]* is:

1, 2, 3, 4, 5, 6, 7, 8, 9, 10, 11, 12

4 Inversions

The maximum number of inversions in a list of length n occurs when the list is in reverse sorted order, and is given by $n^2/2 - n/2$. If $f(n)$ is the number of inversions in completely random data, and $g(n)$ is the number of inversions in the same completely random data but which has been partially sorted, $g(n) / f(n)$ appears constant. Also $f(n) \in O(n^2)$, $g(n) \in O(n^2)$, and $[f(n) - g(n)] \in O(n^2)$.

5 Search

In my next paper, "A recursive binary search algorithm for partially sorted data" (2009), I present an efficient algorithm for searching partially sorted data.

6 Conclusion / summary

An efficient linear time algorithm for partial sorting has been presented. It is appropriate for use on huge lists where sorting is impossible, and is appropriate for real-time applications where sorting is also impossible.

VI. Research Notes

Research Notes

James A. Riechel*

January 9, 2012

1 Some Theory

Define $P(i, j)$ to be the probability that the ith and j^{th} elements in a list of length n are inverted, where $1 \leq i < j \leq n$ and $n \geq 2$.

Assume $P(i, j) = c$, for some constant c, where $0 \leq c \leq 1$.

Define the random variable X:

$$X = \left\{ \begin{array}{ll} 1 & \text{with probability } c \\ 0 & \text{with probability } (1 - c) \end{array} \right.$$

Note that the expected value of X, $E[X]$, is:

$$E[X] = c$$

The number of inversions, $I(n)$, in a list of length n is given by:

$$I(n) = \sum_{i=1}^{n-1} \sum_{j=i+1}^{n} X$$

The expected value of $I(n)$, $E[I(n)]$, is:

$$E[I(n)] = E\left[\sum_{i=1}^{n-1} \sum_{j=i+1}^{n} X \right] = \sum_{i=1}^{n-1} \sum_{j=i+1}^{n} E[X] = \sum_{i=1}^{n-1} \sum_{j=i+1}^{n} c = \frac{cn^2}{2} - \frac{cn}{2}$$

1.1 Conclusion

If the probability that two distinct elements in a list of length n are inverted is non-zero, then the number of inversions in the list is quadratic in n, or $O(n^2)$.

---

*jamesriechel@gmail.com

1.2 Definitions

A list of length n is said to be randomly sorted if and only if $P(i,j) = \frac{1}{2}$, for $1 \le i < j \le n$ and $n \ge 2$, where $P(i,j)$ is the probability that the ith and j^{th} elements are inverted.

A list of length n is said to be fully sorted if and only if $P(i,j) = 0$, for $1 \le i < j \le n$ and $n \ge 2$, where $P(i,j)$ is the probability that the ith and j^{th} elements are inverted.

A list of length n is said to be reverse sorted if and only if $P(i,j) = 1$, for $1 \le i < j \le n$ and $n \ge 2$, where $P(i,j)$ is the probability that the ith and j^{th} elements are inverted.

1.3 Summary

$P(i,j)^a$	Type of list	Exact number of inversions	Expected number of inversions
$0 < c \le 1$	all but fully sorted lists		$\frac{cn^2}{2} - \frac{cn}{2} \in O(n^2)$
0	fully sorted lists	0	
$\frac{1}{2}$	randomly sorted lists		$\frac{n^2}{4} - \frac{n}{4} \in O(n^2)$
1	reverse sorted lists	$\frac{n^2}{2} - \frac{n}{2} \in O(n^2)$	

$^a P(i,j)$ is the probability that the ith and j^{th} elements in a list of length n are inverted, where $1 \le i < j \le n$ and $n \ge 2$.

VII. A fast, space-efficient search algorithm for very, very large files

A fast, space-efficient search algorithm for very, very large files

James A. Riechel[*]

February 28, 2012

Abstract

A fast, space-efficient search algorithm for searching for strings in very, very large files is presented, which is fast and uses virtually no memory. If n is the file size of the input file, and m is the length of the string we are searching for, then in the average case, the time complexity of our search algorithm is $O(n)$, and the space complexity is $O(1)$ (a constant amount of space, not a function of either m or n). If α is the size of our alphabet, our algorithm performs better for larger values of α.

1 Introduction

In this paper we present a search algorithm for searching for strings in very, very large files, especially files that are too large to fit into physical memory. We solve the single-pattern matching problem using a novel approach. The main advantages of our algorithm are: (1) it is appropriate for searching for strings in files, (2) it is fast, and (3) it uses virtually no memory.

We begin by comparing our algorithm to prior work, determining whether or not existing algorithms are appropriate for searching for strings in files, and comparing the average case space and time complexities of each algorithm. Then we consider the worst case, average case, and best case time and space complexities of our search algorithm, and perform two experiments to test our algorithm. We demonstrate our search algorithm with an example, offering the source code for the example in the appendix.

2 Prior work

Let m represent the length of the pattern we are searching for, n represent the file size of our input file, and α represent the size of our alphabet, for $\alpha \geq 2$.

We compare our algorithm to three famous algorithms from the literature. Our algorithm would be classified as an "elementary algorithm," as we do no

---

[*]jamesriechel@gmail.com

preprocessing of the pattern we are searching for. The average case time complexity of our matching algorithm is $O(n)$, which is the same as the other three algorithms, and in the average case, we use only a constant amount of space, or $O(1)$ space. Our algorithm is appropriate for searching files, where you read the file sequentially in order from first byte to last byte, without skipping around, never storing more than the current byte in memory.

The Knuth-Morris-Pratt algorithm [1] is also appropriate for searching files, where you read the file sequentially in order from first byte to last byte, without skipping around, never storing more than the current byte in memory. The Knuth algorithm is a "constructed search engine," because it preprocesses the pattern we are searching for. Preprocessing builds a "partial match" table, also known as a "failure function." This takes $\Theta(m)$ preprocessing time, and $O(m)$ space. The matching portion of the algorithm takes $\Theta(n)$ time in the average and worst cases, which is better than our algorithm, which has a worst case time complexity of $O(mn)$.

The Boyer-Moore string search algorithm [2] is perhaps the most efficient of all the string search algorithms. To adapt this algorithm to search for strings in files, this algorithm would require a buffer of length m, requiring $O(m)$ space. Just like the Knuth algorithm, the Boyer algorithm is a "constructed search engine." The algorithm preprocesses the pattern, building what are sometimes called "jump tables." This requires $\Theta(m + \alpha)$ time, and $O(m + \alpha)$ space. Just like our algorithm, it has an average case matching time complexity of $O(n)$.

The Rabin-Karp string search algorithm [3] can also be adapted to search for strings in files. Again, a buffer would be required, requiring $O(m)$ space. Just like the Knuth and Boyer algorithms, the Rabin algorithm is a "constructed search engine." The algorithm preprocesses the pattern, creating a hash value for the pattern. This requires $\Theta(m)$ time, but requires no more than constant space. It has an average case matching time of $O(n)$, and the same worst case matching time as our algorithm.

Figure 1 compares the average case space and time complexities of the four algorithms, and whether or not they are appropriate for searching for strings in files. Our algorithm has two advantages over the other algorithms presented: (1) our algorithm requires no preprocessing time, and (2) in the average case, we use only a constant, or $O(1)$, amount of space.

3   Algorithm

Our search algorithm reads each byte of the input file one byte at a time, from the first byte of the file to the last byte. It never stores more than the current byte in memory, but is still able to identify all matches of a search string occurring in a file.

The search algorithm uses a linked list to keep track of possible matches. Associated with each node in the linked list is an integer which is an index into the pattern, indicating to what point in the pattern the possible match has matched the pattern thus far.

Algorithm	Appropriate for files	Average case time complexity		Average case space complexity
		Preprocessing time	Matching time	
Our algorithm	Yes	0 (no preprocessing)	$O(n)^a$	$O(1)^a$
Knuth-Morris-Pratt algorithm	Yes	$\Theta(m)$	$\Theta(n)$	$O(m)$
Boyer-Moore string search algorithm	Yes, but with a buffer	$\Theta(m + \alpha)$	$O(n)$	$O(m + \alpha)$
Rabin-Karp string search algorithm	Yes, but with a buffer	$\Theta(m)$	$O(n)$	$O(m)$ (for the buffer)

[a]Assuming each letter in our alphabet is equally likely to occur.

Figure 1: Comparison of four string search algorithms

After each byte is read from the input file, all nodes in the linked list are examined. If the current byte completes a match of the search string, the match is output to the standard output, and the node representing this match is removed from the list. If a possible match in the linked list continues to match the search string, its integer index is incremented. Also, if a possible match in the linked list fails to continue to match the search string, this node is removed from the linked list. Finally, a new node is added to the linked list when the current byte of the input file matches the first byte of the search string. In the source code of our example, we employ a stack data structure to recycle or reuse nodes, to avoid too many and repeated calls to dynamic memory deallocation.

Note that we do not store successful matches in memory. If n is the file size in bytes of the input file, the number of successful matches could be as high as $O(n)$, which would use an unreasonable amount of memory. The advantage of our search algorithm is that it uses virtually no memory at all. Therefore, we output successful matches to the standard output. This output could be redirected to a file, or the source code could be changed to directly write the successful matches to a file.

The source code used in our example is given in the appendix. It is written in C++, but the algorithm could easily be rewritten in any language which supports dynamic memory allocation.

4 Time complexity

Our algorithm does no preprocessing of the search string, and so requires no preprocessing time. Times given in this section are for the worst case, average case, and best case matching times.

Let m represent the length of the string we are searching for, and n represent the file size in bytes of the input file we are searching. We now consider the worst case, average case, and best case matching times of the search algorithm presented. The results are summarized in Figure 2.

4.1 Worst case

At any given time, after each byte is read from the input file, we maintain at most $m - 1$ possible matches in our linked list: one of length 1, one of length 2, and so on, up to one of length $m - 1$. In this worst case, we must visit all $m - 1$ nodes in our linked list for each byte read from the input file. Also, in the worst case, we will add a new node to the linked list for each byte read from the input file. So, in the worst case, we do $m - 1$ visits, and 1 additions, for a total of m operations on our linked list, for each byte read from the input file. Since there are n bytes in the input file, the time complexity of the search algorithm in the worst case is $O(mn)$.

4.2 Average case

We assume that each letter in our alphabet is equally likely to occur. Specifically, if α is the size of our alphabet, we assume that the probability that the next character in our input file is any particular letter in our alphabet is given by $\frac{1}{\alpha}$, for $\alpha \geq 2$. Now define the random variable X_i, for $1 \leq i \leq m-1$:

$$X_i = \begin{cases} 1 & \text{with probability } (\frac{1}{\alpha})^i \\ 0 & \text{with probability } 1 - (\frac{1}{\alpha})^i \end{cases}$$

Note that the expected value of X_i, $E[X_i]$, is:

$$E[X_i] = (\frac{1}{\alpha})^i$$

Now define M_m, the number of possible matches represented in our linked list at any given time.

$$M_m = \sum_{i=1}^{m-1} X_i$$

The expected value of M_m, $E[M_m]$, is:

$$E[M_m] = E\left[\sum_{i=1}^{m-1} X_i\right] = \sum_{i=1}^{m-1} E[X_i] = \sum_{i=1}^{m-1} (\frac{1}{\alpha})^i$$

which is a geometric series with first term $\frac{1}{\alpha}$, and common ratio $\frac{1}{\alpha}$. So:

$$E[M_m] = \frac{1 - (\frac{1}{\alpha})^{m-1}}{\alpha - 1}$$

Since:

$$\lim_{m \to \infty} \frac{1 - (\frac{1}{\alpha})^{m-1}}{\alpha - 1} = \frac{1}{\alpha - 1}$$

It follows that:

$$E[M_m] \leq \frac{1}{\alpha - 1} \leq 1, \text{ for } \alpha \geq 2.$$

Note that $E[M_m]$ is a constant, and not a function of m.

So, on average, after each new byte is read from the input file, we have one node or less in our linked list to visit. Doing so takes a constant amount of time. Since there are n bytes in the input file, it follows that the average case running time of our search algorithm is $O(cn)$, for some constant c. Since the constant does not matter, the average case running time is $O(n)$.

Case	Time complexity
Worst case	$O(mn)$
Average case	$O(n)$
Best case	$O(n)$

Figure 2: Time complexity of our search algorithm (matching times)

4.3 Best case

In the best case, we read the entire input file of length n, and never encounter even one possible match, not even of length 1. But we must still read the entire input file, so the best case running time of our algorithm is $O(n)$.

5 Space complexity

Again, let m represent the length of the string we are searching for, and n represent the file size in bytes of the input file we are searching. We now consider the worst case, average case, and best case space complexity of the search algorithm presented. We are only interested in the number of nodes in our linked list. We ignore the constant amount of memory required by the search algorithm. The results are summarized in Figure 3.

5.1 Worst case

At any given time, after each byte is read from the input file, we maintain at most $m - 1$ possible matches in our linked list: one of length 1, one of length 2, and so on, up to one of length $m - 1$. Therefore, our linked list never stores more than $m - 1$ nodes. Thus, the space complexity of the search algorithm in the worst case is $O(m - 1)$, or $O(m)$.

5.2 Average case

From section 4.2 (above), we know that:

$$E[M_m] \leq \frac{1}{\alpha - 1} \leq 1, \text{ for } \alpha \geq 2$$

where M_m is the number of possible matches represented in our linked list at any given time. The expected value of M_m, $E[M_m]$, is a constant less than or equal to one. It is not a function of m. Therefore, in the average case, we store a small and constant number of nodes in our linked list. Thus, the space complexity in the average case is $O(c)$, for some constant c. But since constants do not matter, the space complexity in the average case is $O(1)$.

Case	Space complexity
Worst case	$O(m)$
Average case	$O(1)$
Best case	$O(0)$

Figure 3: Space complexity of our search algorithm

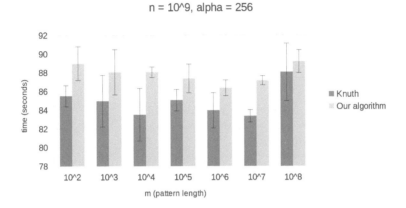

n = 10^9, alpha = 256

Figure 4: First experiment

5.3 Best case

In the best case, we read the entire input file of length n, and never encounter even one possible match, not even of length 1. Since no possible matches are encountered, no new nodes are ever added to the linked list. So, in the best case, the space complexity is $O(0)$.

6 Experiments

We perform two experiments to test our search algorithm in comparison to itself and to Knuth's algorithm.

In the first experiment, n and α are held constant, and m, the length of the pattern, is varied from 10^2 to 10^8 in powers of 10. We search for a completely random pattern of length m in a completely random file composed of 256 different characters. Figure 4 summarizes the results.

The mean times in seconds is plotted on the y-axis, and the error bars show a 95% confidence interval of the sample mean, assuming execution times are normally distributed. When the error bars for Knuth's algorithm and our algorithm overlap, statistically there is no difference in execution time. This happens in 4 out of 7 cases. In the other three cases, Knuth's algorithm is statistically faster.

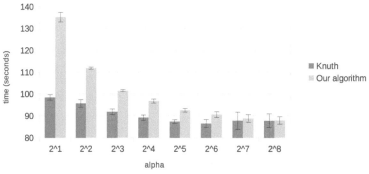

Figure 5: Second experiment

In the second experiment, m and n are held constant, and α, the size of our alphabet, is varied from 2^1 to 2^8 in powers of 2. We search for a completely random pattern of length 100 in a completely random file composed of α different characters. Figure 5 summarizes the results.

Again, the mean times in seconds is plotted on the y-axis, and the error bars show a 95% confidence interval of the sample mean, assuming the execution times are normally distributed. Again, when the error bars for Knuth's algorithm and our algorithm overlap, statistically there is no difference in execution time. This occurs for $\alpha = 128$ and $\alpha = 256$. For other values of α, the Knuth algorithm is statistically faster.

Our algorithm is sensitive to the value of α. Larger α reduces the average number of nodes stored in our linked list. Linked lists use dynamic memory, and are expensive to maintain.

7 An example

In file format, the human genome is organized into chromosomes: one file for each chromosome. Each chromosome file contains a very long sequence of nucleotides: an "A" represents Adenine, a "G" represents Guanine, a "C" represents Cytosine, and a "T" represents Thymine. Figure 6 shows the beginning of the second human chromosome of a particular human being.

As an example, we search this human being's second chromosome for a marker of length 14: "CCTACCCTAACCCT". So, for this search task, $m = 14$, n is approximately 238.2 megabytes, and $\alpha = 4$. The output of the program is given in Figure 7. There are three matches at positions 1, 1383 and 225118504.

```
CCTACCCTAACCCTAACCCTAACCCTAACCCTAACCCTAACCCTAACCCTAACCCTAACCCTAACCCTAA
CCCTAACCCTAACCCTAACCCTAACCCTAACCCTAACCCTAACCCTAACCCTAACCCTAACCCTAACCCT
AACCCTAACCCTAACCCTAACCCTAACCCTAACCCTAACCCTAACCCTAACCCTAACCCTAACCCTAACC
CTAACCCTAACCCTAACCCTAACCCTAACCCTAACCCTAACCCTAACCCTAACCCTAACCCTAACCCTAA
CCCTAACCCTAACCCTAACCCTAACCCTAACCCTAACCCTAACCCTAACCCTAACCCTAACCCTAACCCT
AACCCTAACCCTAACCCTAACCCTAACCCTAACCCTAACCCTAACCCTAACCCTAACCCTAACCCTAACC
CTAACCCTAACCCTAACCCTAACCCTAACCCTAACCCTAACCCTAACCCTAACCCTAACCCTAACCCTAA
CCCTAACCCTAACCCTAACCCTAACCCTAACCCTAACCCTAACCCTAACCCTAACCCTAACCCTAACCCT
AACCCTAACCCTAACCCTAACCCTAACCCTAACCCTAACCCTAACCCTAACCCTAACCCTAACCCTAACC
CTGACCCTAACGCTAACCCTAACCCTAACCCTAACCCTAACCCTAACCCTAACCCTAACCCTAACCCTAA
CCCTAACCCTAACCCTAACCCTAACCCTAACCCTAACCCCAACCCTAACCCTAACCCTA
ACCCTAACCCTAACCCTAACCCTAACCCTAACCCTAACCCTAACCCTAACCCTAACCCTAACCCTAACCC
TAACCCTAACCCTAACCCTAACCCTAACCCTAACCCTAACCCTAACCCTAACCCTAACCCTAACCCTAAC
CCTAACCCTAACCCTAACCCTAACCCTAACCCTAACCCTAACCCTAACCCCTAACCCTAACCCT
AACCCTAACCCTAACCCTAACCCTAACCCTAACCCTTAACCCTTAACCCTAACCCTAACCCTAACCCTAA
CCCTAACCCCTAACCCTAACCCTAACCCTAACCCTGGGCGTAACGCTAACCCTAAGGCTAGCCC
TAACCCTAACCGGAAGCCGAACGCGGACCGTAACCCTAACCCTAACCCTAACCCTAACCCTAACCCTAAC
CCTAACCCTAACCCTAACCCTAACCCTAACCCTAACCCTAACCCTAACCCTAACCCTAACCCTAACCCTA
ACCCTAACCCTAACCCTAACCCTAACCCTAACCCTAACCCTAACCCTAACCCTAACCCTAACCCTAACCC
TAACCCTAACCCTAACCCTAACCCTAACCCTAACCCTAACCCTAACCCTAACCCTACCCTAACCCTAACC
CTAACCCTAACCCCTAACCCTAAGCCGAAGCCTAACTCGTGTCTGACTTTGAGTATTCAGTGCTGCAAAC
AGGAAGTATTTTATTCACCGTCGATGCGGCCCCGAGGGGTCCCAAAGCGAGGCAGTGCCCCCAAACTCTG
TCCTGAGGAGAATGCTGCTTCGCCTTTACGGTGTCCACCGGGTGTGTGCTCAGCAAAACGCAGCTCCGCC
...
...
...
```

Figure 6: The beginning of a particular human being's second chromosome

```
MATCH position 1
MATCH position 1383
MATCH position 225118504
```

Figure 7: Program output: search results for "CCTACCCTAACCCT"

8 Conclusion

We believe there might be a need for search algorithms that can search for strings in very, very large files, especially files that cannot fit into physical memory. These search algorithms should be fast and space-efficient, at least in the average case. One such algorithm has been presented.

Since the worst case and best case time and space complexities are unlikely ever to occur in practice, the performance of our algorithm depends on its average case performance. If m is the length of the string we are searching for, and n is the file size in bytes of the input file we are searching, then the average case time complexity of our search algorithm is $O(n)$, and the average case space complexity is $O(1)$.

If α is the size of our alphabet, we note that our search algorithm performs better for larger values of α, because when α is larger the average number of nodes in our linked list is smaller, lowering the overhead associated with dynamic memory management. Also, in theory, our search algorithm should perform well versus other algorithms when m is larger, since we do no preprocessing of the search string.

References

[1] Donald Knuth; James H. Morris, Jr. "Fast pattern matching in strings." SIAM Journal on Computing, 6 (2), pp. 323-350, 1977.

[2] R. S. Boyer; J. Strother Moore. "A fast string searching algorithm." Communications of the Association for Computing Machinery, 20 (10), pp. 762-772, 1977.

[3] Karp, RM; Rabin, MO. "Efficient randomized pattern-matching algorithms." IBM Journal of Research and Development, 31 (2), pp. 249-260, March 1987.

A Source code

The source code for the example is written in C++, but the search algorithm could easily be rewritten in any language that supports dynamic memory allocation. The source code is divided into two types of files: header files whose filenames end in ".h", and source code files whose filenames end in ".c++". Figures 8 and 9 show "node.h" and "node.c++". Figures 10 and 11 show "stack.h" and "stack.c++". Figures 12, 13 and 14 show "list.h" and "list.c++". Figures 15, 16 and 17 show "search.h" and "search.c++". Finally, Figure 18 shows "main.c++".

```
class possiblematch { // a node in our linked list

    private:

        possiblematch* previous;
        possiblematch* next;
        int matched; // index to matched position (so far)

    public:

        possiblematch();
        void setprevious(possiblematch*);
        void setnext(possiblematch*);
        void setmatched(int);
        int getmatched();
        possiblematch* getprevious();
        possiblematch* getnext();
};
```

Figure 8: "node.h"

```
#include<stdio.h>
#include "node.h"

possiblematch::possiblematch() {

    previous = NULL;
    next = NULL;
    matched = -1;
}

void possiblematch::setprevious(possiblematch* p) {

    previous = p;
}

void possiblematch::setnext(possiblematch *n) {

    next = n;
}

void possiblematch::setmatched(int m) {

    matched = m;
}

int possiblematch::getmatched() {

    return (matched);
}

possiblematch* possiblematch::getprevious() {

    return (previous);
}

possiblematch* possiblematch::getnext() {

    return (next);
}
```

Figure 9: "node.c++"

```
#include "node.h"

class possiblematchstack { // our memory management

    private:

        possiblematch* top;

    public:

        possiblematchstack(); // constructor
        ~possiblematchstack(); // deconstructor
        possiblematch* pop(); // stack pop operator
        void push(possiblematch*); // stack push operator
};
```

Figure 10: "stack.h"

```
#include<stdio.h>
#include "stack.h"

possiblematchstack::possiblematchstack() {

    top = NULL;
}

possiblematchstack::~possiblematchstack() {

    possiblematch* next;
    while (top != NULL) {
        next = top->getnext();
        delete(top);
        top = next;
    }
}

possiblematch* possiblematchstack::pop() {

    if (top == NULL) {
        return (new(possiblematch));
    }
    possiblematch* oldtop;
    oldtop = top;
    top = oldtop->getnext();
    return (oldtop);
}

void possiblematchstack::push(possiblematch* pmatch) {

    if (pmatch != NULL) {
        possiblematch* oldtop;
        oldtop = top;
        top = pmatch;
        top->setnext(oldtop);
    }
}
```

Figure 11: "stack.c++"

```
#include "stack.h"

class possiblematchlist {

    private:

        possiblematch* front;
        possiblematch* back;
        possiblematchstack stack;

    public:

        possiblematchlist();
        ~possiblematchlist();
        possiblematch* getfront();
        void addpossiblematch(int);
        void removepossiblematch(possiblematch*);
};
```

Figure 12: "list.h"

```
#include<stdio.h>
#include "list.h"

possiblematchlist::possiblematchlist() {

   front = NULL;
   back = NULL;
}

possiblematchlist::~possiblematchlist() {

   while (front != NULL) {
      removepossiblematch(front);
   }
}

possiblematch* possiblematchlist::getfront() {

   return (front);
}

void possiblematchlist::addpossiblematch(int m) {

   possiblematch* pmatch;
   pmatch = stack.pop();
   pmatch->setmatched(m);
   if (back == NULL) { // new node is only node in list
      front = pmatch;
      back = pmatch;
      pmatch->setprevious(NULL);
      pmatch->setnext(NULL);
   } else { // there's at least one node already in the list
      back->setnext(pmatch);
      pmatch->setprevious(back);
      back = pmatch;
      pmatch->setnext(NULL);
   }
}
```

Figure 13: "list.c++"

```
void possiblematchlist::removepossiblematch(possiblematch* pmatch) {

    possiblematch* p;
    possiblematch* n;

    p = pmatch->getprevious();
    n = pmatch->getnext();

    if (p != NULL) { // node is not the first in the list
        p->setnext(n);
    } else { // node is the first in the list
        front = n;
    }

    if (n != NULL) { // node is not the last in the list
        n->setprevious(p);
    } else { // node is the last in the list
        back = p;
    }

    stack.push(pmatch);
}
```

Figure 14: "list.c++" (continued)

```
#include<stdio.h>

void search(FILE*, char*, int);
```

Figure 15: "search.h"

```
#include "list.h"
#include "search.h"

void search(FILE* fp, char* marker, int markerlength) {

    if (markerlength <= 0) return;
    possiblematchlist pmatchlist;
    unsigned long long int position = 0;

    while (!feof(fp)) {

        char c;
        fscanf(fp, "%c", &c);

        if (c != '\n') { // skip newlines in chromosome file

            position = position + 1;
            possiblematch* pmatch;
            pmatch = pmatchlist.getfront();

            while (pmatch != NULL) {

                int matched;
                matched = pmatch->getmatched();

                if (c == marker[matched]) { // it continues to match

                    pmatch->setmatched(matched + 1);

                    if ((pmatch->getmatched()) == markerlength) { // complete match

                        printf("MATCH position %lld\n", position - markerlength + 1);
                        possiblematch* temp;
                        temp = pmatch->getnext();
                        pmatchlist.removepossiblematch(pmatch);
                        pmatch = temp;
```

Figure 16: "search.c++"

```
        } else { // not a complete match

            pmatch = (pmatch->getnext());
        }

    } else { // it no longer matches

        possiblematch* temp;
        temp = pmatch->getnext();
        pmatchlist.removepossiblematch(pmatch);
        pmatch = temp;
    }
}

if (c == marker[0]) { // if we should start a new possible match

    if (markerlength == 1) {

        printf("MATCH position %lld\n", position); // trivial case

    } else {

        pmatchlist.addpossiblematch(1);
    }

}
            }
        }
    }
    fclose(fp);
}
```

Figure 17: "search.c++" (continued)

```
#include "search.h"

main() {

    FILE* fp;
    fp = fopen("chr2", "r");
    char marker[256] = "TAATCTATACAAACCA";

    search(fp, marker, 16);
}
```

Figure 18: "main.c++"

VIII. A new extremely fast pseudo-random number generator

A new extremely fast pseudo-random number generator

James Alan Riechel

January 22, 2013

Abstract

An extremely fast pseudo-random number generator is presented which requires three (3) seeds, and only four (4) integer operations to generate the next pseudo-random number. One of the three (3) seeds can be zero (0), and the other two seeds are generated using someone else's pseudo-random number generator. The pseudo-random number generator requires only two (2) integer additions, one (1) integer modulus, and one (1) integer increment to generate the next pseudo-random number.

IX. The world's first linear-time sorting algorithm!

The world's first linear-time sorting algorithm!

James Alan Riechel

January 22, 2013

Abstract

Two linear-time algorithms are presented which fully sort perfectly randomly sorted lists. We assume these perfectly randomly sorted lists were generated using the random sorting algorithms presented in our previous article[1]. By definition, a perfectly randomly sorted list of length n has $n^2/4 - n/4$ inversions. After executing the given algorithms, the list becomes fully sorted again with exactly zero (0) inversions. Both algorithms execute in linear time. In order words, if the perfectly randomly sorted list is of length n, both algorithms require $O(n)$ time to execute, restoring the list to fully sorted order.

James A. Riechel, "Two new random sorting algorithms," 2012.

X. Two new random sorting algorithms

Two new random sorting algorithms

James Alan Riechel

January 22, 2013

Abstract

Two linear-time algorithms are presented which convert a fully sorted list into a perfectly randomly sorted list. A perfectly randomly sorted list is defined as a list that has exactly one-half ($\frac{1}{2}$) of the possible number of inversions in a list. A list of length n can have no more than $n^2/2 - n/2$ inversions. A perfectly randomly sorted list has exactly half ($\frac{1}{2}$) this number of inversions, namely: $n^2/4 - n/4$. Both algorithms execute in linear time. In other words, if the list is of length n, both algorithms execute in $O(n)$ time, producing perfectly randomly sorted lists.

XI. Recursive binary search for partially sorted data

Recursive binary search for partially sorted data

James Alan Riechel

June 3, 2013

Abstract

We present an efficient search algorithm which is appropriate for searching data that is either partially sorted or fully sorted. The algorithm presented is robust. It works on all five types of lists: reverse sorted, unsorted, perfectly randomly sorted, partially sorted, and fully sorted. If we assume the key we are searching for can be found in a list of length n, the time complexity of our algorithm is $O(\sqrt[i]{n})$ for $i \geq 1$. Again, if the search key can be found in our list, and if the list is fully sorted, our algorithm has the same time complexity as regular binary search, i.e. $O(\lg n)$. If the search key cannot be found in our list, or if the list is in reverse sorted order, the algorithm presented has a time complexity of $O(n)$.

1 Introduction

Despite its simple expression in algorithmic form (it looks very similar to regular old binary search), the search algorithm presented is perhaps the most important search algorithm in ten (10) or twenty (20) years, and the first search algorithm designed specifically to search data that is partially sorted. In the very worst cases, the algorithm presented takes no more than linear or $O(n)$ time to find a key in a list of length n. In better cases (for example, when the key is in the list, and the list is in partially sorted order), the algorithm presented has fantastic sublinear performance, i.e., $O(rad\ n)$.

k-selection algorithm	Time complexity
Selection algorithm plus pivot (first/last k not sorted)	$O(n)$
Self-balancing binary search tree	$O(n \log k)$
Binary heap and priority queue	$O(n + k \log k)$
Quicksort-based (first/last k sorted)	$O(n + k \log k)$
Quicksort-based (first/last k unsorted)	$O(n)$
Tournament algorithm	$O(n + k \log n)$

Figure 1: Time complexity of several k-selection algorithms

2 Prior Work

To our best knowledge our search algorithm is the very first specifically designed for searching data that has been partially sorted. There are really no other similar search algorithms to compare our algorithm to. However, there is a large body of work in what is called "partial sorting" [1]. All of these partial sorting algorithms are also known as "k-selection algorithms." These algorithms find the k-smallest or the k-largest in a list of length n. The result is a list which has been partially sorted.

Figure 1 shows the time complexity of some but not all k-selection algorithms as a function of n and k as previously defined. With the exception of the tournament algorithm, if we assume k is constant and independent of n, all of these k-selection algorithms have a time complexity of $O(n)$. Similarly, the tournament algorithm has a time complexity of $O(n + \log n)$.

3 Algorithm

We refer to our algorithm as "Recursive binary search for partially sorted data", or "rbspsd" for short. Sample C code for our algorithm is given in Figure 2. To search for a key in a list of length n, a call to $rbspsd(data, key, 0, n-1)$ is made.

In regular binary search, you only have to search one branch (either the left branch or the right branch). In our algorithm, since we do not assume the list is fully sorted, we might need to search both branches (both the left and the right).

```
int rbspsd(int* data, int key, int n1, int n2) {

    if (n2 < n1) return -1;
    int m = ((int) ((n2 - n1 + 1) / 2)) + n1;
    if (key == data[m]) return m;
    int result;
    if (key < data[m]) {
        if ((result = rbspsd(data, key, n1, m - 1)) != -1) return result;
        if ((result = rbspsd(data, key, m + 1, n2)) != -1) return result;
    }
    else { // key > data[m]
        if ((result = rbspsd(data, key, m + 1, n2)) != -1) return result;
        if ((result = rbspsd(data, key, n1, m - 1)) != -1) return result;
    }
    return -1;
}
```

Figure 2: Recursive binary search for partially sorted data, *rbspsd()*

4   Time complexity

We now present a recursive formula for $T(n)$, the expected number of comparisons recursive binary search for partially sorted data performs when searching a list of length n. First some base cases:

$$T(0) = 0$$

$$T(1) = 1$$

In other words, it takes zero (0) comparisons to search a list of length zero (0), and it takes one (1) comparison to search a list of length one (1).

We assume the key we are searching for can be found in our list. Also assume p is the probability of choosing the correct branch while searching (either the left branch or the right branch), and $(1 - p)$ is the probability of having to search both branches (both the left and the right). Note that p is an experimentally obtained constant. Also assume n is large, and that $n = 2^k$, for $k \in \{0, 1, 2, ...\}$.

$$T(n) = p\, T(n/2) + (1 - p)\, 2\, T(n/2) + 1$$

$$T(n) = 2\ T(n/2) - p\ T(n/2) + 1$$

$$T(n) = (2 - p)\ T(n/2) + 1$$

We close this recursive formula:

$$T(n) = \sum_{i=0}^{\lg n} (2 - p)^i$$

Define $k = (2-p)$. The dominating or highest-order term of $T(n)$ is $k^{\lg n}$, so $O(T(n)) = O(k^{\lg n})$. Now $k^{\lg n} = n^{1/(\log_k 2)} = \sqrt[\log_k 2]{n}$. Define $i = \log_k 2$. Finally, since $0 \le p \le 1$ and $1 < k \le 2$:

$$O(T(n)) = O(\sqrt[i]{n}), \text{ for } i \ge 1$$

In plain English, the time complexity of recursive binary search for partially sorted data is the ith root of n, where n is the length of the list, and i is any number greater than or equal to one.

In the worst case, when $i = 1$, the algorithm is linear, i.e. $O(n)$. In the best case, the algorithm approaches $O(\log n)$, the time complexity of regular binary search.

Now we present a table of p, k, i, and $O(T(n))$ values:

p	Type of list	k	i^*	$O(T(n))$
0.0	reverse sorted	2.0	1	$O(n)$
0.1	unsorted	1.9	1.08	$O(\sqrt[1.08]{n})$
0.2	unsorted	1.8	1.18	$O(\sqrt[1.18]{n})$
0.3	unsorted	1.7	1.31	$O(\sqrt[1.31]{n})$
0.4	unsorted	1.6	1.47	$O(\sqrt[1.47]{n})$
0.5	perfectly randomly sorted	1.5	1.71	$O(\sqrt[1.71]{n})$
0.6	partially sorted	1.4	2.06	$O(\sqrt[2.06]{n})$
0.7	partially sorted	1.3	2.64	$O(\sqrt[2.64]{n})$
0.8	partially sorted	1.2	3.80	$O(\sqrt[3.80]{n})$
0.9	partially sorted	1.1	7.27	$O(\sqrt[7.27]{n})$
1.0	fully sorted	1.0	undefined	$O(\lg n)$

* Rounded to the nearest hundredth

5   Conclusion / Summary

A new type or class of algorithm has been presented for searching for a key in a list of length n, which has a time complexity of $O(\sqrt[i]{n})$, for $i \ge$

1, if the search key can be found in our list. The best search algorithm has always been regular binary search which has a time complexity of $O(\lg n)$, but unfortunately regular binary search assumes the list which we are searching is fully sorted. Our algorithm makes no such assumption, and will work on any type of list. It just performs better on lists which have been partially sorted, and will have the same time complexity as regular binary search on fully sorted lists, if we assume the key we are searching for is in our list. In the worst cases where either the search key is not in our list, or when the list is in reverse sorted order, our algorithm has a time complexity of $O(n)$.

6   References

[1] J.M. Chambers (1971). Partial sorting. CACM 14(5):357-358.

XII. World's first constant-time search algorithm!

World's first constant-time search algorithm!

James Alan Riechel

June 19, 2013

Abstract

An efficient search algorithm is presented which requires constant or $O(1)$ time to execute, if we assume the search key we are searching for can be found among the k smallest or k largest elements in a list of length n. We also assume k is constant and independent of n. It is not necessary for the search key to appear in the list, but if it does, it is assumed to be among the k smallest or k largest. If the search key appears in the list, but is not among the k smallest or k largest, the algorithm produces a "false negative," indicating that the search key does not appear in the list when in fact it does. We first employ a k-selection algorithm, so that the list begins with the k smallest, or ends with the k largest. They are two types of k-selection algorithms. In the first type, the k smallest or the k largest appearing at the start or the end of the list appear in unsorted order. In the second type, the k smallest appear at the start of the list in sorted order, or the k largest appear at the end of the list in sorted order. Both types of k-selection algorithms require $O(n)$ time, if we assume k is constant and independent of n. You get to choose which k-selection algorithm to use. Next, depending on your choice of k-selection algorithm, you use either simple linear search (if the first or last k appear in unsorted order) or binary search (if the first or last k appear in sorted order) to search for our search key in the first or last k elements in the list. This requires either $O(k)$ or $O(\log k)$ time, but since we assume k is constant and independent of n, this portion of the algorithm requires constant or $O(1)$ time to complete. Instead of simple linear search or binary search, you can employ a more advanced search algorithm such as "recursive binary search for partially sorted data," which would require $O(\sqrt[i]{k})$ for $i \geq 1$ time to complete. This search algorithm works whether the first or last k elements appear in unsorted or sorted order. Again, since k is constant and independent of n, this approach would complete in $O(1)$ time. The algorithm presented can even call itself recursively using a sublist comprised of the first or last k elements of the list, and a new value of k, say k_2, where $k_2 < k$. This would require $O(k)$ time to complete, but since both k and k_2 are constant and independent of n and each other, it would require only $O(1)$ time to complete. We can perform any number of these searches after we employ our k-selection algorithm. This is not unreasonable. Take, for example, binary search, which only works on lists that have been fully sorted. After fully sorting a list, you can use binary search any number of times until the list needs to be fully sorted again. Likewise, we can employ the search portion of our algorithm any number of times before our list becomes "disturbed," and it is necessary to perform another k-selection algorithm on the list. It is probably even possible to implement some list operations which do not disturb the order of the list after the k-selection algorithm completes.

XIII. Another constant-time search algorithm

Another constant-time search algorithm

James Alan Riechel

June 27, 2013

Abstract

We present an efficient search algorithm that requires constant or $O(1)$ time to execute, if we assume the search key we are searching for can be found among the k_1 oldest elements (primacy), or among the k_2 newest elements (recency), or both, in a list of length n. We also assume that k_1 and k_2 are constant and independent of n, and we assume that associated with each element in the list is a date/time stamp that allows us to partially sort the list in chronological order. The search key does not have to appear in the list, but if it does, it is assumed to be among the k_1 oldest elements, or among the k_2 newest elements, or both. If the search key appears in the list, but is not among the k_1 oldest or k_2 newest (or both), the algorithm returns a "false negative," indicating that the search key does not appear in the list when in fact it does. Using the date/time stamps of elements in the list, we first employ a k-selection algorithm or algorithms to place the k_1 oldest elements at the start of the list, or the k_2 newest elements at the end of the list, or both. Since k_1 and k_2 are constant and independent of n, this requires linear or $O(n)$ time to complete. Next, we employ simple linear search to search for our search key among the k_1 oldest elements, or the k_2 newest elements, or both. This takes at most $O(k_1+k_2)$ time to complete, but since k_1 and k_2 are constant and independent of n, this portion of the algorithm takes constant or $O(1)$ time to complete. The constant-time search portion of our algorithm can be performed any number of times until the established partial chronological order of the list becomes "disturbed," and we need to perform another k-selection algorithm or algorithms on the list using the date/time stamps of the elements in the list, as described above.

XIV. Introducing the first recursive binary search algorithm for partially sorted data

Project Summary

A fundamental problem in computer science is to search a list of length n for a search key. Traditional approaches such as binary search [1, 2] and simple linear search [2] assume the list is in fully sorted order, or do not take advantage of the fact that the list might be partially ordered. The best search algorithm has always been binary search which has logarithmic or $O(\lg n)$ time complexity, but unfortunately binary search requires that the list be in fully sorted order. In general, fully sorting a list takes log-linear or $O(n \lg n)$ time [1, 2].

We will present a robust search algorithm which works on any type of list and does take advantage of the fact that the list might be partially ordered. The list can be reverse sorted, unsorted, perfectly randomly sorted, partially sorted, or fully sorted, terms which we will define later. If a list is partially sorted, our search algorithm has fantastic sub-linear performance.

We will present the theory of our search algorithm to show that the average case time complexity of our algorithm is given by $\Theta(\sqrt[i]{n})$ for $i \geq 1$, and that the worst case time complexity of our algorithm is given by $\Theta(n)$. The best case time complexity of our algorithm is given by $\Theta(\lg n)$. We will perform a number of experiments to confirm and explore our theoretical results, comparing our search algorithm to other algorithms. Our objective is to do a fair theoretical and experimental comparison between our search algorithm and other search algorithms, employing mathematics to derive our theoretical results, and employing computers to test and analyze our algorithm.

Intellectual Merit

A new type or class of search algorithm will be presented that works on any type of list. The algorithm can have amazing sub-linear performance. Its average case time complexity is $O(\sqrt[i]{n})$ for $i \geq 1$, which falls in-between linear or $O(n)$ time and logarithmic or $O(\lg n)$ time. The authors understand that the classical problem of search in computer science has been considered "solved." We suggest there is room for new ideas.

Broader Impacts

Fully sorting lists in $O(n \lg n)$ time just so you can use binary search to search in $O(\lg n)$ time is wasteful in terms of time, electricity, and money. Our search algorithm will work on any type of list: the list does not need to be sorted first. Our algorithm does perform better when the list is already partially sorted, but if not, you can partially sort a list in linear or $O(n)$ time using a k-selection algorithm [3] or alternative algorithm, if you assume k is constant and independent of n. The potential to save time, electricity, and money is enormous.

Project Description

1 Introduction

We present an advanced search algorithm which is probably the most important search algorithm in ten (10) or twenty (20) years. Our algorithm is particularly useful for searching lists that are partially ordered, though the algorithm is robust and will work on any type of list. It can have amazing sub-linear performance, and is theoretically no slower than simple linear search in the worst cases. If our grant proposal is funded, we promise to complete the theoretical time-complexity analysis of our algorithm, and perform and analyze experiments to test and compare our algorithm to other algorithms.

2 Prior Work

To our best knowledge, our advanced search algorithm is the first specifically designed to search lists that might be partially ordered. Our algorithm is robust, too. It will work on any type of list. The two most important algorithms to compare our work to are binary search [1, 2] and simple linear search [2]. Binary search has always been the best search algorithm, but it assumes the list is in fully sorted order. A comparison with simple linear search is also important, since simple linear search has low overhead, and should execute quickly even if it does not take advantage of the fact that the list might be partially ordered.

3 Algorithm

Our advanced search algorithm is given in Figure 1 in Dijkstra notation. Our algorithm appears similar to binary search, but exhibits entirely different average-case time complexity behavior than binary search (see Theory section below).

	int search($list$, key, n_1, n_2)
1	if $n_2 < n_1$ then return -1
2	$m \leftarrow \lfloor \frac{n_2 - n_1 + 1}{2} \rfloor + n_1$
3	if $key = list[m]$ then return m
4	if $key < list[m]$ then
5	$\quad result \leftarrow$ search($list$, key, n_1, $m - 1$)
6	$\quad$ if $result \neq -1$ then return $result$
7	$\quad$ return search($list$, key, $m + 1$, n_2)
8	else
9	$\quad result \leftarrow$ search($list$, key, $m + 1$, n_2)
10	$\quad$ if $result \neq -1$ then return $result$
11	$\quad$ return search($list$, key, n_1, $m - 1$)

Figure 1: Our advanced search algorithm

If our algorithm does not find what it is looking for at the current node or element in the list, it makes a recursive call on one of its branches (line 5 or 9) based on a comparison (line 4). If it also fails to find what it is looking for in this branch, it recurses on the other branch (line 7 or 11) before returning. Possibly checking both branches is necessary since we do not assume the list is in fully sorted order. The list can be in any order.

4   An Example

Figure 2 shows an example of searching for the number '2' in a list of length 7. The list is given by $\{12, 4, 3, 7, 2, 16, 11\}$.

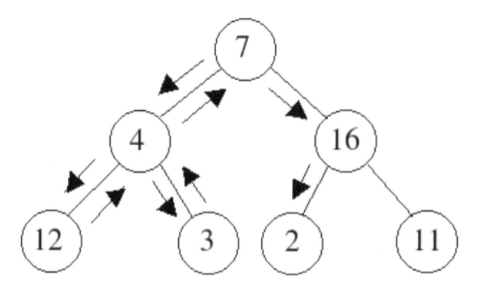

Figure 2: An example: searching for '2' in a list of length 7

5   Theory

In the theory that follows, we refer to the probability p, the probability of choosing the correct branch while searching. For a given list of length n, the probability p is computed as follows:

$$p = 1 - \frac{\text{Number of inversions in list}}{\text{Maximum number of inversions in list}}$$

The value of p characterizes the type of list we are searching. Figure 3 shows these characterizations.

p	Type of list
$p = 0.0$	Reverse-sorted
$0.0 < p < 0.5$	Unsorted
$p = 0.5$	Perfectly randomly sorted
$0.5 < p < 1.0$	Partially sorted
$p = 1.0$	Fully sorted

Figure 3: Characterization of list by p-value

We will now discuss the average-case, worst-case, and best-case time complexities of our advanced search algorithm.

5.1 Time Complexity

Assume $T(n)$ is the expected number of comparisons required to search a list of length n using our advanced search algorithm. Also, assume p is the probability of choosing the correct branch while searching, and $(1 - p)$ is the probability of having to search both branches. Also define $k = (2 - p)$, and $i = \log_k 2$.

5.1.1 Average-case Performance

We will rigorously prove that if the search key can be found in the list, the average-case time complexity of our advanced search algorithm is as given in Figure 4.

Type of list	Average-case time complexity
all lists (key in list)	$T(n) = \Theta(\sqrt[i]{n})$, for $i \geq 1$

Figure 4: Average-case time complexity of our advanced search algorithm

5.1.2 Worst-case Performance

There are two worst cases, both with the same worst-case time complexity. First, a worst case results if the search key is in the list, but the list is in reverse-sorted order. Second, a worst case results if the search key is not in the list. In either case, we will rigorously prove that the worst-case time complexity of our advanced search algorithm is as given in Figure 5.

Type of list	Worst-case time complexity
reverse-sorted (key in list)	$T(n) = \Theta(n)$
all lists (key not in list)	$T(n) = \Theta(n)$

Figure 5: Worst-case time complexity of our advanced search algorithm

5.1.3 Best-case Performance

A best case results when the search key is in the list, and the list is in fully sorted order. In this case, our advanced search algorithm has the same time complexity as binary search. See Figure 6.

Type of list	Best-case time complexity
fully sorted (key in list)	$T(n) = \Theta(\lg n)$

Figure 6: Best-case time complexity of our advanced search algorithm

6 Experiments to Perform

We will perform two types of experiments.

6.1 First experiment

In our first set of experiments, we will choose a search key that is in the list, and vary p from 0.0 to 1.0, comparing our algorithm to simple linear search for different values of n.

6.2 Second experiment

In our second set of experiments, we will choose a search key that is not in the list, and hold p fixed or constant at 0.5, again comparing our algorithm to simple linear search for different values of n.

6.3 How to create a partially sorted list

A k-selection algorithm [3] can be used to partially sort a list of length n in linear or $O(n)$ time, if you assume k is constant and independent of n. We will present an alternative partial sorting algorithm that also partially sorts in linear or $O(n)$ time, and does not require the choice of a parameter k.

Continued on next page...

7 Expected Experimental Results

Figure 7 presents a table showing $\Theta(T(n))$ values for different values of p, using the definitions of p and $T(n)$ given in the Theory section.

p	Type of list	k	i^*	$\Theta(T(n))$
0.0	reverse sorted	2.0	1	$\Theta(n)$
0.1	unsorted	1.9	1.08	$\Theta\left(\sqrt[1.08]{n}\right)$
0.2	unsorted	1.8	1.18	$\Theta\left(\sqrt[1.18]{n}\right)$
0.3	unsorted	1.7	1.31	$\Theta\left(\sqrt[1.31]{n}\right)$
0.4	unsorted	1.6	1.47	$\Theta\left(\sqrt[1.47]{n}\right)$
0.5	perfectly randomly sorted	1.5	1.71	$\Theta\left(\sqrt[1.71]{n}\right)$
0.6	partially sorted	1.4	2.06	$\Theta\left(\sqrt[2.06]{n}\right)$
0.7	partially sorted	1.3	2.64	$\Theta\left(\sqrt[2.64]{n}\right)$
0.8	partially sorted	1.2	3.80	$\Theta\left(\sqrt[3.80]{n}\right)$
0.9	partially sorted	1.1	7.27	$\Theta\left(\sqrt[7.27]{n}\right)$
1.0	fully sorted	1.0	undefined	$\Theta(\lg n)$

* Rounded to the nearest hundredth

Figure 7: Expected experimental results of our advanced search algorithm

Continued on next page...

Figure 8 shows a contour plot that describes our algorithm's theoretical performance. The horizontal axis is n, the length of the list. The vertical axis is p, as defined in the Theory section. The third dimension, represented in color, is $T(n)$, also defined in the Theory section. Based on Figure 8, you can tell that our algorithm is faster for smaller n and larger p. This is intuitive. A shorter list is faster to search, and a larger value of p means you will find what you are looking for quicker. The algorithm is slower for larger value of n and smaller values of p. This is also intuitive. Longer lists take more time to search, and a smaller value of p means it will take longer to find what you are looking for.

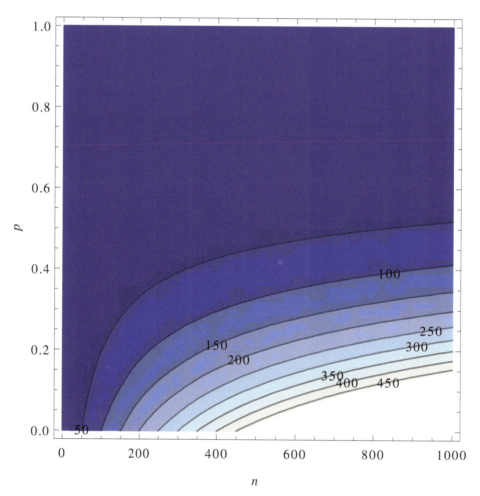

Figure 8: Theoretical performance of our advanced search algorithm

Continued on next page...

Figure 9 also shows a plot that describes our algorithm's theoretical performance. Again, the horizontal axis is n, the length of the list, and the vertical axis is time in the abstract measured in comparisons. The top-most curve in blue is the slowest, and is based on a p-value of 0.0. It is a straight line. Then below this blue curve, each successive curve has an increased p-value of 0.1, except for the bottom curve which is barely just above the horizontal axis. It has a p-value of 0.99. The point of the graph is to show that our advanced search algorithm is sub-linear. All the curves representing p-values greater than 0.0 fall below the top-most blue curve which is linear.

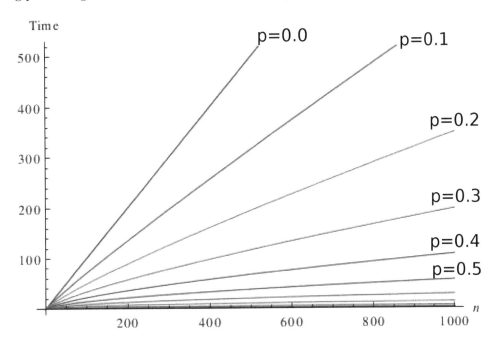

Figure 9: Theoretical performance of our advanced search algorithm

8 Comparison of our advanced search algorithm

Figure 10 compares our advanced search algorithm to binary search and simple linear search. Binary search is superior when the list is already fully sorted. Our algorithm is superior when the list is already partially sorted, but not fully sorted. Simple linear search has the same worst-case time complexity as our algorithm, but does not take advantage of the fact that the list might be partially ordered in the average-case.

algorithm	sorting or partial sorting time	average-case search time	worst-case search time
binary search	$O(n \lg n)$, if necessary	$O(\lg n)$	$O(\lg n)$
simple linear search	N/A (not applicable)	$O(n)$	$O(n)$
our algorithm	$O(n)$, if necessary	$\Theta(\sqrt[i]{n})$, for $i \geq 1$	$\Theta(n)$

Figure 10: Comparison of three algorithms

8.1 Simple linear search versus our algorithm

Figure 11 shows at least theoretically when our advanced search algorithm is faster than simple linear search. The horizontal axis is n, and the vertical axis is p, both as previously defined. Our algorithm is usually faster, especially for larger values of n and p.

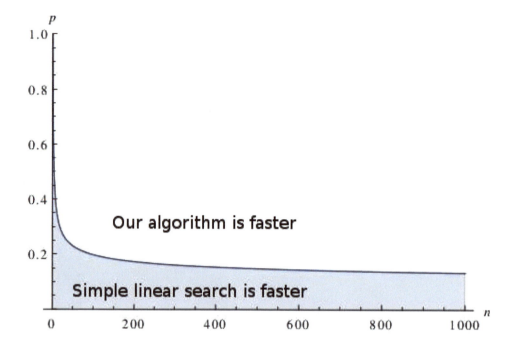

Figure 11: Comparison of simple linear search and our algorithm

Continued on next page...

8.2 Quicksort and binary search versus partial sort and our advanced search algorithm

Figure 12 shows a theoretical comparison between using Quicksort [1, 2] followed by binary search to search a list, versus using a linear-time partial sorting algorithm followed by our advanced search algorithm to search a list. The horizontal axis is n, the length of the list. The vertical axis is time in the abstract measured in comparisons. The upper line in blue shows the time required to Quicksort followed by binary search. The lower line in red shows the time required to partially sort the list followed by our algorithm. Under these circumstances, it is clear that linear-time partial sorting followed by our algorithm is faster than the alternative.

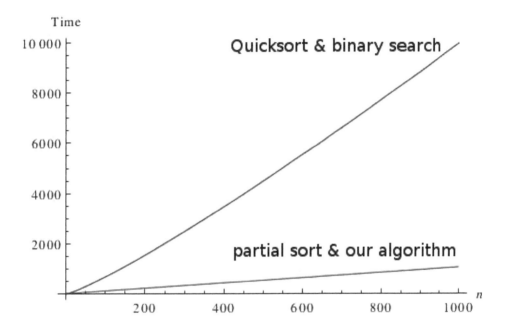

Figure 12: Quicksort and binary search versus partial sorting and our algorithm

9 Summary

If our project is funded, we will complete the theoretical and experimental work of our project. In the theoretical work, we will rigorously prove the average-case, worst-case, and best-case time complexities using Θ-notation. In the experimental work, we will show for what values of n and p (as previously defined) our algorithm is superior to simple linear search. We will also present an alternative partial sorting algorithm that does not require the selection of a parameter k as is necessary in k-selection algorithms.

Broader Impacts

We will show that our advanced search algorithm is more often than not superior to simple linear search, depending on the value of p as previously defined. We will also show that doing a partial sort followed by our algorithm is superior to using Quicksort and binary search. In both of these cases, there is a huge savings in execution time involved in searching and possibly sorting or partially sorting. This savings in time translates to a savings in money and electricity. Super computers, for example, are extremely expensive to run and operate. They require a huge amount of electricity, and electricity is expensive, and are otherwise expensive to maintain.

References Cited

[1] Thomas H. Cormen, Charles E. Leiserson, Ronald L. Rivest, Introduction to Algorithms, pages 246-248 (binary search), pages 172-174 (lower bounds for sorting), pages 153-171 (Quicksort), 1990.

[2] Donald E. Knuth, The Art of Computer Programming, Volume 3 / Sorting and Searching, pages 406-414 (binary search), pages 393-402 (sequential search), pages 181-195 (minimum-comparison sorting), pages 114-123 (Quicksort), 1973.

[3] *Partial sorting*, https://en.wikipedia.org/wiki/Partial_sorting.

XV. *rbspsd()* scaled to supercomputers

$rbspsd()^{\star}$ scaled to supercomputers

J. Riechel*

257 S. De Lacey Ave., Unit 1128, Pasadena, CA 91105

H. York**

Abstract

Previously, we presented a new search algorithm which we sometimes referred to as 'recursive binary search for partially sorted data,' or *rbspsd()*. Here, we scale this algorithm to supercomputers. We begin by describing how the algorithm might be scaled to supercomputers. Next, we explore the average-case, worst-case, and best-case time complexities of the supercomputer-scaled algorithm. Finally, we present the theoretical speedup of the supercomputer-scaled algorithm in the average, worst, and best cases.

Keywords: parallel search algorithm, search algorithm, parallel algorithm, parallel search, supercomputer, supercomputing

☆Recursive binary search for partially sorted data

*Corresponding author

**Editor

Email addresses: jamesriechel@gmail.com (J. Riechel), info@heather-york.com (H. York)

URL: sites.google.com/site/jamesriechel (J. Riechel), www.heather-york.com (H. York)

1. Introduction

On a single-processor computer, the best search algorithm has always been binary search. Unfortunately, binary search requires that the list be in fully sorted order, and sorting is expensive (because it takes a lot of time). A good alternative algorithm is simple linear search, also known as linear search or sequential search. Simple linear search executes quickly because it has low overhead, but, unfortunately, it does not exploit the fact that the list might be partially ordered.

2. Prior work

We previously presented an algorithm that does not require a fully sorted list, and does exploit the fact that the list might be partially ordered [1, 2]. We sometimes referred to this algorithm as 'recursive binary search for partially sorted data,' or *rbspsd()* for short.

3. Algorithm

We present the serial algorithm and one (1) possible parallel implementation.

3.1. Serial algorithm

We previously presented the serial version of our algorithm for one (1) processor [1, 2]. Check Appendix A for this algorithm.

3.2. Parallel algorithm

We now discuss one possible parallel implementation of our algorithm, in which there are k child processors and one (1) parent processor.

3.2.1. Child processors

Each of k child processors, $1 \leq j \leq k$, executes the following statement:

$$rbspsd(list, key, \frac{(j-1)n}{k}, \frac{jn}{k} - 1)$$

We are assuming n is a multiple of k.

When the child processor's search is complete, it returns its result to the parent processor.

3.2.2. Parent processor

The parent processor waits for the first child to find a match, and then returns this match to the calling process or processor. If all child processors return -1 ("search key not found"), the parent processor returns a -1 to the calling process or processor.

4. Time complexity

Assume n is the length of the list, and k is the number of nodes or processors in the supercomputer accomplishing a common search task. Also, without loss of generality, assume n is a multiple of k. Define $T(n,k)$ to be the expected number of comparisons required to search for a search key in a list of length n using k processors or nodes in a supercomputer.

4.1. Average case

Values of k and n	Average-case time complexity
any k, any n	$T(n,k) = \Theta(\sqrt[i]{\frac{n}{k}})$, for $i \geq 1$
k constant and independent of n	$T(n,k) = \Theta(\sqrt[i]{n})$, for $i \geq 1$
$\lim_{k \to n_-}$	$T(n,k) = \Theta(1)$

4.2. Worst case

Values of k and n	Worst-case time complexity
any k, any n	$T(n,k) = \Theta(\frac{n}{k})$
k constant and independent of n	$T(n,k) = \Theta(n)$
$\lim_{k \to n_-}$	$T(n,k) = \Theta(1)$

4.3. Best case

Values of k and n	Best-case time complexity
any k, any n	$T(n,k) = \Theta[\lg(\frac{n}{k} + 1)]$
$k = 1$	$T(n,k) = \Theta[\lg(n + 1)]$
$\lim_{k \to n_-}$	$T(n,k) = \Theta(1)$

5. Speedup

Speedup is a measure of how much faster a parallel algorithm will execute as processors or nodes are added to a computation. If S_p is the speedup of an algorithm using p processors, and T_1 is the time the algorithm takes on one (1) processor, and T_p is the time the algorithm takes on p processors:

$$S_p = \frac{T_1}{T_p}$$

We now introduce the speedup of our supercomputer-scaled algorithm, giving different speedup values for the average, worst, and best cases. Again, n is the length of the list we are searching, and k is the number of nodes or processors cooperating together to accomplish a common search task. Proofs of these speedups can be found in Appendix B.

Case	Speedup
Average	$\Theta(\sqrt[i]{k})$, for $i \geq 1$
Worst	$\Theta(k)$
Best	$\Theta[\frac{\log(n+1)}{\log(n+k)-\log k}]*$

* Note that the best-case speedup is not independent of n.

A typical value of i is $i = 2$, so in the average case, the speedup when $k = 100$ would be about 10, and the speedup when $k = 10{,}000$ would be about 100.

6. Conclusion / Summary

We have presented how our search algorithm might be parallelized on a supercomputer. We have discussed the average-case, worst-case, and best-case time complexities of our search algorithm when scaled to supercomputers. We have presented the speedup of our algorithm running on a supercomputer in the average, worst, and best cases, providing proofs of these speedups in Appendix B.

Conclusion: Oddly enough, the best speedup is achieved in the worst case. We received an 'average' amount of speedup in the average case. And, oddly enough, the worst speedup is achieved in the best case.

References

[1] James A. Riechel, *Introducing the first recursive binary search algorithm for partially sorted data*, `http://tinyurl.com/m8johc6`, 2013.

[2] James A. Riechel, *Recursive binary search for partially sorted data*, `http://tinyurl.com/lrg7tpf`, 2013.

Appendix A. Serial algorithm

Here we present the serial version of our algorithm for one (1) processor. To search a *list* of length n for a search key *key*, a call to $rbspsd(list, key, 0, n-1)$ is made.

	int rbspsd($list$, key, n_1, n_2)
1	if $n_2 < n_1$ then return -1
2	$m \leftarrow \lfloor \frac{n_2 - n_1 + 1}{2} \rfloor + n_1$
3	if $key = list[m]$ then return m
4	if $key < list[m]$ then
5	$\quad result \leftarrow$ rbspsd($list$, key, n_1, $m-1$)
6	$\quad$ if $result \neq -1$ then return $result$
7	$\quad$ return rbspsd($list$, key, $m+1$, n_2)
8	else
9	$\quad result \leftarrow$ rbspsd($list$, key, $m+1$, n_2)
10	$\quad$ if $result \neq -1$ then return $result$
11	$\quad$ return rbspsd($list$, key, n_1, $m-1$)

Serial version of our algorithm for one (1) processor.

Appendix B. Proofs

Here, we prove the average-case, worst-case and best-case theoretical speedups of our parallelized algorithm. We assume $n > 0$ or $n \geq 1$, $1 \leq k \leq n$, and that T_1 is the expected number of comparisons on one (1) processor, and T_k is the expected number of comparisons on k processors. Also, S_k is the theoretical speedup using k processors expressed in Θ-notation. Finally, we assume n is a multiple of k.

Appendix B.1. Average-case speedup

An average case occurs when the search key is in the list. The list can be in any order.

Theorem B.1 1. *The theoretical speedup of our parallelized algorithm in the average case is given by $S_k = \Theta(\sqrt[i]{k})$, for $i \geq 1$, where k is the number of nodes or processors being used in the supercomputer.*

PROOF OF THEOREM B.1 1. We know from previous work [1, 2] and from work presented here that $T_1 = \Theta(\sqrt[i]{n})$, and $T_k = \Theta(\sqrt[i]{n/k})$, for $i \geq 1$. Specifically, if we ignore constants, and assume $n = 2^r$ and $n/k = 2^s$ for $r \geq 0$ and $s \geq 0$, we know that:

$$T_1 = \sqrt[i]{n} + \sqrt[i]{n/2} + \sqrt[i]{n/4} + \cdots + 1$$

and

$$T_k = \sqrt[i]{n/k} + \sqrt[i]{n/2k} + \sqrt[i]{n/4k} + \cdots + 1$$

Factoring we get:

$$T_1 = \sqrt[i]{n}(1 + \sqrt[i]{1/2} + \sqrt[i]{1/4} + \cdots + \sqrt[i]{1/n})$$

and

$$T_k = \sqrt[i]{n/k}(1 + \sqrt[i]{1/2} + \sqrt[i]{1/4} + \cdots + \sqrt[i]{k/n})$$

Let $a = (1 + \sqrt[i]{1/2} + \sqrt[i]{1/4} + \cdots + \sqrt[i]{1/n})$, and $b = (1 + \sqrt[i]{1/2} + \sqrt[i]{1/4} + \cdots + \sqrt[i]{k/n})$. a and b are both constants since $\sqrt[i]{1/n}$ and $\sqrt[i]{k/n}$ are both numbers between 0 and 1. Therefore:

$$S_k = T_1/T_k = (a\sqrt[i]{n})/(b\sqrt[i]{n/k}) = a/b\sqrt[i]{k} = \Theta(\sqrt[i]{k})$$

$\square$

Appendix B.2. Worst-case speedup

There are two worst cases. In the first, the search key is not in the list. In the second, the list is in reverse-sorted order.

Appendix B.2.1. Worst-case speedup #1

In this worst case the search key does not appear in the list.

Theorem B.2.1 1. *The theoretical speedup of our parallelized algorithm in the worst case when the search key does not appear in the list is given by $S_k = \Theta(k)$, where k is the number of nodes or processors being used in the supercomputer.*

PROOF OF THEOREM B.2.1 1. In this case each processor must examine every element in its list. Therefore:

$$T_1 = n$$

and

$$T_k = n/k$$

The theoretical speedup is given by:

$$S_k = T_1/T_k = n/(n/k) = k = \Theta(k)$$

$\square$

Appendix B.2.2. Worst-case speedup #2

In this worst case the list is in reverse-sorted order.

Theorem B.2.2 1. *The theoretical speedup of our parallelized algorithm in the worst case when the list is in reverse-sorted order is given by $S_k = \Theta(k)$, where k is the number of nodes or processors being used in the supercomputer.*

PROOF OF THEOREM B.2.2 1. In this case each processor must examine roughly half the elements in its list:

$$T_1 = (n+1)/2$$

and

$$T_k = (n/k+1)/2$$

The theoretical speedup is given by:

$$S_k = T_1/T_k = \frac{(n+1)/2}{(n/k+1)/2} = \frac{n+1}{n/k+1} = \frac{n+1}{(n+k)/k} = k(\frac{n+1}{n+k})$$

Now note that $(n+1)/(n+k)$ is a number between $1/2$ and 1. Therefore:

$$\frac{1}{4}k \leq k(\frac{n+1}{n+k}) \leq 2k$$

So, $S_k = \Theta(k)$. □

Appendix B.3. Best-case speedup
    A best case occurs when the list is in fully sorted order, and the search key can be found in the list.

Theorem B.3.1 1. *The theoretical speedup of our parallelized algorithm in the best case when the list is in fully-sorted order and the search key is in the list is given by $S_k = \Theta(\frac{\log(n+1)}{\log(n+k)-\log k})$, where k is the number of nodes or processors being used in the supercomputer, and n is the length of the list.*

PROOF OF THEOREM B.3.1 1. If $n = 2^i - 1$, then at most i comparisons are required to search a list of length n on a single-processor computer. If $n/k = 2^j - 1$, then at most j comparisons are required to search lists of length n/k on each of k nodes or processors in a supercomputer. So:

$$T_1 = i$$

and

$$T_k = j$$

Now:

$$S_k = T_1/T_k = i/j = \frac{\lg(n+1)}{\lg(n/k+1)} = \frac{\lg(n+1)}{\lg\frac{n+k}{k}} = \frac{\lg(n+1)}{\lg(n+k) - \lg k}$$

Or:

$$S_k = \frac{\log(n+1)}{\log(n+k) - \log k} = \Theta(\frac{\log(n+1)}{\log(n+k) - \log k})$$

□

www.ingramcontent.com/pod-product-compliance
Lightning Source LLC
Chambersburg PA
CBHW041420050326
40689CB00002B/586